WriteTraits®
STUDENT TRAITBOOK

Vicki Spandel • Jeff Hicks

GREAT SOURCE®
EDUCATION GROUP
A Houghton Mifflin Company

Vicki Spandel

Vicki Spandel was codirector of the original teacher team that developed the six-trait model and has designed instructional materials for all grade levels. She has written several books, including *Creating Writers—Linking Writing Assessment and Instruction* (Longman), and is a former language arts teacher, journalist, technical writer, consultant, and scoring director for dozens of state, county, and district writing assessments.

Jeff Hicks

Jeff Hicks has over 17 years of teaching experience in grades two through nine. Until recently, Jeff taught seventh- and eighth-grade English and math on a two-person teaching team, focusing on the reading/writing connection through six-trait writing activities. Currently, Jeff is a full-time writer and presenter.

Design/Production: Bill Westwood/Andy Cox, David Drury

Illustration: Jim Higgins, Mark DaGrossa, Scott Van Buren, Chris Vallo

Proofreading/Editorial: Erik Martin/Judy Bernheim, Alex Culpepper

Cover: Illustration by Claude Martinot Design

Printed in the United States of America

International Standard Book Number: 978-0-669-49039-8
International Standard Book Number: 0-669-49039-3

10 11 12 13 14 - 1689 - 15 14 13 12

Contents

Unit 4: Word Choice

Unit 5: Sentence Fluency

Unit 6: Conventions

Warm-up Activity 1

Ranking Three Papers

Read the three pieces of writing that follow. Decide which piece is strongest, which piece is next strongest, and which piece is weakest. All three papers are informational papers about the polar bear.

Sample 1

Polar bears are interesting creatures. They are mammals. In fact, they are among the largest of all North American land mammals. Polar bears are often considered dangerous.

The polar bear lives in the North Country, near the North Pole. This is where it gets its name. For many years, polar bears were hunted by native people of the region for food and for their white fur, which is highly valued. Today, they are no longer hunted for fear of extinction. Sometimes, though, one is shot because it is terrorizing a village. As you can see, the polar bear is one of the most interesting but dangerous creatures on Earth.

Sample 2

Polar bears live in the North, where it is normally very cold. They have thick fur, so they can stand the cold. Polar bears grow to a huge size and live mostly on seals and other things they hunt. They do hibernate for part of the year. The mother polar bear has one or two cubs, and she teaches them to hunt and is very protective of them. The polar bear has a lot of fat on its body, called blubber. This is what keeps it warm during the winter. If it gets too hot in the summer, the polar bear will look for shade to keep itself cool. Polar bears grow to a huge size and are the largest of all bears. They have very white fur, so they blend right into the snow.

Sample 3

Have you ever looked at a picture of a frozen arctic wilderness and wondered whether anything could live there? In fact, quite a few creatures call this formidable land home. One of them is the polar bear, which is quite at home in the arctic. How does the polar bear do it?

Few people realize what a skilled swimmer the polar bear is. It can swim rapidly and for long periods, even diving quite deep under the water as necessary to sneak up on an unsuspecting seal basking in the sun on an ice floe. It is the only bear that dives to hunt. The polar bear is equally menacing on top of the ice. Its whitish fur makes it all but invisible to its potential prey. Only its eyes and the very tip of its nose are black, and the bear will remain still for long periods to avoid being seen.

It is easy to look at the polar bear and appreciate its size and strength. What is less obvious is the cunning of this wily creature, which hunts with the resourcefulness of an old woodsman. It is a creature that loves winter best, thriving in a cold and icy habitat for most of the year.

Share Your Thoughts

Discuss the papers with your partner. Then, together, fill in each blank with the number of the sample (1, 2, or 3) that fits best. Be sure to add your reasons.

The strongest paper is Sample ____ because _____

_____.

The next strongest is Sample ____ because _____

_____.

The weakest paper is Sample ____ because _____

_____.

Ideas

Unit 1

By now, you're experienced enough as a writer to know that writing is mostly about ideas. The thing about ideas, though, is that they can be like plain, unworked cookie dough. Plain old cookie dough, sitting there doing nothing, is just the beginning. The dough has potential, of course. Eventually, you can make cookies from the dough, but you have to work at it. You have to cut, shape, and bake the cookie dough. Finally, when the cookies are done, you can arrange them on a plate. In a sense, this is the process your ideas go through to become a focused piece of writing. They must be worked and shaped to become a final product.

This unit is about planning your writing so that your ideas interest your reader. You'll learn about

◆ two prewriting techniques (drawing and listing details)

◆ narrowing your topic

◆ turning unclear writing into focused writing

◆ using details to hold the reader's attention

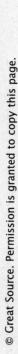

name: .... date: ....

Draw on the Count of Three

Writers do a lot of things to warm up, or "prewrite." Some writers discuss ideas with friends. Some writers make lists. Some writers even draw pictures. Now, you may not think of yourself as an artist, but drawing is a great way to kick-start your thinking. So once you have a topic in mind, drawing can help you think of details you didn't even know were in your head.

Getting Off to an Energetic Start

For many writers, finding a topic is the hardest part of the writing process. It's easier when you care about the topic, have something definite to say, and feel confident about your knowledge. It's also easier to choose a topic when you've done some prewriting. Consider this example topic: "Fun in the Great Outdoors." First, imagine what you would write about this topic. Then, answer the following questions.

What image do you get when you think of "fun in the great outdoors"?

Write it here: _____

_____

_____

_____

1. Do you think everyone in your class would think of the same thing?   **Yes   No**

2. Consider this list—boating, hiking, camping, hunting, fishing, birdwatching, cycling, rafting, sailing, rock climbing, skateboarding. Does it cover everything you would need to write about the topic?   **Yes   No**

3. Would you be ready to write about this topic without any further thought?   **Yes   No**

You probably answered **No** to that last question, and that's OK. What you need is a prewriting strategy to help you warm up.

Picture It in Your Head—Then, Draw It on Paper

Go back to your answer to the question, "What image do you get when you think of 'fun in the great outdoors'?" Use the space below to draw a quick and simple picture of what popped into your head, such as people, places, actions, and weather.

Look closely at your picture. Here are some things for you to think about: What kinds of details did you include? Does your picture show a specific place on a specific day? Did you include people? Who are they? What are they doing? What's the weather like? Use the space below to give your picture a title that describes what your picture is generally about. (Examples— *Trout Fishing on Timothy Lake, Central Park in Winter, Antelope Hunting After School*)

Title: _____

Do you know what you have just done? You've helped bring your topic into focus, and you've recorded some important details you'll need to create a clear picture for your readers. Before you write, though, here's another important step— thinking about the supporting details. This time, we'll use a connected but slightly different prewriting strategy.

Labeling the Bricks (Another Prewriting Trick)

Think of all the details you put into your drawing as the bricks you use to build a big idea for your readers. Label the bricks in your stack with a few key words that tell about important parts of your picture. There are six bricks to help you keep the topic manageable. Try to fill all six. (Yes, you can add more bricks if you need them.)

Build It for Your Readers

It's now time to use those detail bricks to build a piece of writing. Look at your title and your stack of bricks. Which brick holds the most interesting detail? That brick will provide a good place to begin. On a separate sheet of paper, turn those brick details into sentences that make word pictures for your audience.

Share and Compare

Share your writing with a partner. Listen carefully for specific details that relate to your partner's title.

A Writer's Question

Do you think drawing a picture and then creating a stack of detail bricks are steps you could do by yourself? (Remember, it's *not* important how well you can draw; it's important to use drawing to help you think through your idea.)

_____ **I had trouble drawing everything I pictured in my head.**

_____ **I still need practice, but I think I can do this. A picture made it easier to write.**

_____ **I found drawing pretty simple; I'm ready to use this on my own.**

name: .... date: ....

Narrowing Your Topic

Did you ever get one of those writing assignments that just seemed so huge? For example, "Sports" or "History of the Western United States"? If you're like most writers, you found that big topic hard to manage. Surprisingly, many young writers assign themselves big topics like these— even when they have a choice. Working with a too-big topic makes getting started very frustrating. It's like trying to find a street in Riverton, Wyoming, by looking at a map of the world.

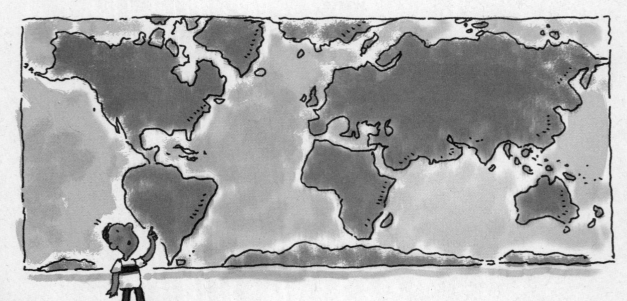

Listening to Your Inner Navigator

Writers need to ask themselves questions. As a writer, you can narrow a big topic by talking to your inner navigator. Use questions that start with these basic words: **Who, What, When, Where, Why, How,** and **Which.** Your answers will take you from a big, sprawling topic to one that's manageable. Here's an example:

Which Way to Topicville?

Topic: Sports

Inner Navigator: **What** do you really want to say about sports?

Writer's Answer: I want to say that I'd rather play a sport than watch one.

Are we in Topicville yet?   _____ Yes   **X** No

Topic: Sports I can play

Inner Navigator: OK, **which** sports are your favorites?

Writer's Answer: Well, any team sports played outside.

Are we in Topicville yet?   _____ Yes   **X** No

Topic: Team sports I can play outside

Inner Navigator: **What** particular outdoor team sport do you like?

Writer's Answer: Lacrosse.

Are we in Topicville yet?   _____ Yes   **X** No
(But we're close!)

Topic: Lacrosse

Inner Navigator: **What** do you like about lacrosse?

Writer's Answer: There is quite a lot to like—the action, the equipment, the history, and it's really fun.

Are we in Topicville yet?   _____ Yes   **X** No
(But the good news is we're only one question away!)

Topic: <u>Things I like best about the game of Lacrosse</u>

Inner Navigator: **Which** one of those things—action, equipment, history, fun—do you most want to write about?

Writer's Answer: I think I'll start with the history of the sport and how it was first played by Native Americans.

Have we arrived in Topicville?   __X__ Yes   _____ No
                                              (Absolutely!)

Final topic: <u>Linking Lacrosse to Native American Culture</u>

You're the Navigator, So You Ask the Questions

Where do "inner navigator" questions come from? They come from you, of course. So it's time now to grab the map, ask the questions, and steer yourself to Topicville. When you think you've reached Topicville, write your final topic on the line provided.

Some Navigating Tips: Start with a general topic (such as *food, pets, school*). Then, begin asking yourself some questions— **What** would I want everyone to know about this topic? **What** is it I really like about this topic? You may be able to drive into Topicville after only 1 or 2 questions, or you might need 5 or 6. Use as many questions as you need.

Topic: _____

Inner Navigator's Question: _____

Writer's Answer: _____

Are we in Topicville yet?   _____ Yes   _____ No

Topic: _____

Inner Navigator's Question: _____

Writer's Answer: _____

Are we in Topicville yet?   _____ Yes   _____ No

name: .... date: ....

Topic: _____

Inner Navigator's Question: _____

Writer's Answer: _____

Are we in Topicville yet?   _____ Yes   _____ No

Topic: _____

Inner Navigator's Question: _____

Writer's Answer: _____

Are we in Topicville yet?   _____ Yes   _____ No

Topic: _____

Inner Navigator's Question: _____

Writer's Answer: _____

Are we in Topicville yet?   _____ Yes   _____ No

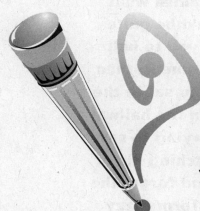

A Writer's Question

What are the benefits for you as the writer and your audience if you try to narrow your topic before you get too far into the writing?

Benefits for the Writer	Benefits for the Audience

name: .... date: ....

From Fuzzy to Focused

Suppose a friend asked you this question: "Would you mind getting that thing down from the whatchamacallit, checking it out, then putting the old whosiewhatsit in that other space-like area?" Would you have *any* idea what you were supposed to do? Chances are you'd be quite surprised to learn that your friend wanted you to help move a piano from an upstairs apartment, tune it, then load it onto a truck. As that out-of-tune piano sat in the apartment, you'd be scratching your head in the hallway, wondering what on earth your friend was trying to say. As a writer, you can leave your reader scratching his or her head, too—if you use fuzzy language and forget the details. Don't worry, though—you can transform fuzzy writing into focused writing.

Sharing an Example: Esperanza Rising

Let's take a look at a passage from Pam Muñoz Ryan's book. Notice how she provides details of characters and actions to describe the scene.

Papa handed Esperanza the knife. The short blade curved like a scythe, its fat wooden handle fitting snugly in her palm. This job was usually reserved for the eldest son of a wealthy rancher, but since Esperanza was an only child and Papa's pride and glory, she was always given the honor. Last night she had watched Papa sharpen the knife back and forth across a stone, so she knew the tool was edged like a razor.

"Cuidate los dedos," said Papa. "Watch your fingers."

. . . The clusters were heavy on the vine and ready to deliver. Esperanza's parents, Ramona and Sixto Ortega, stood nearby, Mama, tall and elegant, her hair in the usual braided wreath that crowned her head, and Papa, barely taller than Mama, his graying mustache twisted up at the sides. He swept his hand toward the grapevines, signaling Esperanza. When she walked toward the arbors and glanced back at her parents, they both smiled and nodded, encouraging her forward. When she reached the vines, she separated the leaves and carefully grasped a thick stem. She put the knife to it, and with a quick swipe, the heavy cluster of grapes dropped into her waiting hand. Esperanza walked back to Papa and handed him the fruit. Papa kissed it and held it up for all to see.

"¡La cosecha!" said Papa. "Harvest!"

Pam Muñoz Ryan, *Esperanza Rising.* (New York: Scholastic, 2000), pp. 4–6

What Can You See?

The author, Pam Muñoz Ryan, creates a clear picture for her readers. True, you may still have some questions, but the author has already told you a lot about the characters and events of the story. What specific words did the author use to paint this picture? Complete the chart with specific words from the passage that helped put a picture in your mind.

Person, Place, Thing, Event	Words That Helped You See
knife	*short blade . . .*
Esperanza	
Mama	
Papa	
grapes	
importance of cutting grapes	

Share and Compare

Share your chart with several classmates. As you see and hear what others wrote, feel free to add any details you may have missed.

What Did the Author Do?

What if Pam Muñoz Ryan had written these sentences in place of the passage above:

> *Her father handed her the knife. She cut the grapes and handed them to him.*

What is missing in this new, shorter version? Put a check by anything you feel is missing.

- clear, precise word choice _____
- clear, descriptive phrases _____
- things I can picture in my mind _____
- setting or character details _____
- sensory details _____

There's a good chance you checked more than one item from the list. Why? Because the things on the list are the very things writers use to create clear pictures for readers. The "revised" version does not do that. This time, let's start with a piece of fuzzy writing, and you can add the details.

From Fuzzy to Focused in a Flash

This piece of fuzzy writing needs your help. Read it once. Then close your eyes and try to picture what the author is writing about. When you have done that, read it again with a pencil in your hand. Circle any words that should be replaced. Make notes in the margins to remind yourself what details should be added. Finally, revise the writing as you see fit, moving it from fuzzy to focused.

Fuzzy Writing:

This time his car broke down on the road. The weather was bad, and he would have to walk. He was going to be late for work, and his boss would be mad. He felt pretty bad.

Focused Writing:

_____

_____

_____

_____

_____

_____

_____

_____

_____

A Writer's Question

Look back at your revision, and check each of the following changes that matches something you did to improve the writing.

_____ **I changed some words to make the writing clearer.**

_____ **I added sensory details (sights, sounds, smells, feelings).**

_____ **I added dialogue.**

_____ **I added descriptive writing to make a picture in the reader's mind.**

_____ **I added some strong verbs.**

Put a _second check_ by each kind of change you think you might try in the future.

name: .... date: ....

That's Pretty Sketchy!

Have you ever had a television show interrupted by a news report? The announcer teases you with a hint of a big news story then leaves you hanging with the promise of "More to come later!" Of course, the television network hopes the audience will stay tuned. Some might, but many viewers will grow bored and change the channel or turn off the television. Without really meaning to, writers sometimes force their audiences to make similar choices about "staying tuned." If a piece of writing is too sketchy, a reader may have to work too hard to fill in the blank spots. Some readers aren't willing to make the effort, so they just tune out. If you want to keep your audience tuned in, hold their attention with some sharp details!

"Stay Tuned" or "Change Channels"?

Read the following samples. As you read, try to visualize the writer's idea. Are you getting a clear picture? Or is the writer's idea still too sketchy? Decide whether you would "stay tuned" (that is, keep reading the piece) or whether you would "change channels" and give up on it. Then, in the space provided after each sample, mark your choice and briefly describe the reasons behind your choice.

Sample 1

My Dog

I live in a tall apartment building in a big city. The elevator ride usually leaves my stomach feeling wobbly. We're allowed to have pets, but there are a lot of rules about what we can and can't do. I have to be careful. I have a dog. I've always loved dogs, and my dog is special. In my apartment building, there are all kinds of pets including snakes, ferrets, cats, and fish. Almost everyone loves my dog.

How do you feel? Check one.

_____ Way too sketchy—change channels now!

_____ I'll give it a minute—it might get better.

_____ I'll definitely stay tuned. This story is terrific!

My Thoughts (reasons for your choice):

_____

_____

_____

_____

Sample 2

All About My Brother

Tanner is my brother. Actually, he's my younger brother. I can't call him my little brother, because he's almost as tall as I am. He's got red hair and glasses, and a cast on his arm. I guess I'm partly responsible for the cast. Tanner is always hungry; he eats more than I do. He's really good at playing computer games, which is his favorite thing to do after school.

How do you feel? Check one.

_____ I'm bored—change channels now!

_____ I'll give it a minute—this could improve any second.

_____ I'll definitely stay tuned. This story is a winner!

My Thoughts:

_____

_____

_____

_____

Sample 3

The Secret Woods

The last time we were at the beach, my mom and I hiked along a trail we always take. Suddenly, though, where we usually go left, for some reason we headed right. To the left were these awesome, rolling sand dunes; to the right was the great unknown, at least to us. The trail followed the ridge of this sandy hill, then cut sharply down to a thick, dark grove of trees we had never noticed before. All along the trail were deer tracks—and another animal track we did not recognize. Some of the tracks seemed very fresh.

We hesitated a moment at the edge of the trees and then followed the tracks inside. The first thing we noticed was how eerily quiet it was. We couldn't even hear the ocean anymore.

How do you feel? Check one.

_____ This is putting me to sleep—change channels now!

_____ I'm not giving up just yet—I see a glimmer of hope.

_____ I'm definitely staying tuned. I want to see what happens next.

My Thoughts:

_____

_____

_____

Time to Revise

Select one of the two samples that you rated as being "too sketchy." Revise it to include the details needed to make the main idea clear and well supported.

_____

_____

_____

_____

_____

A Writer's Question

How do writers invite readers inside their ideas and keep them tuned in? Write down three specific things you or your partner did as you revised.

Organization

As a writer, you have lots of information to share with your readers. The trouble is, no matter how terrific your ideas might be, readers may not be able to make sense of them or may not find them interesting unless you organize them properly.

Why is organization so important? Well, think of a calendar with the dates out of order. How handy would that be? The same goes for writing. You would never give a friend out-of-order directions for finding your house. Yet, when writing is poorly organized, writers are sending readers on the same kind of wild chase. Make sure your writing lets readers find their way to your main idea.

In this unit, you'll find ways to organize your writing to make sure that your reader understands it. You'll learn about

◆ seven patterns for organizing information

◆ using the right pattern for the right purpose

◆ using transition words

◆ writing an organized paragraph

name: .... date: ....

Name That Pattern!

Whether you are writing the recipe for your grandma's famous turkey noodle soup, a newspaper story about a high school basketball team, or a description of the Grand Canyon at sunrise, you need a plan for organizing your ideas. You may have great information and an eye for details, but without an organizational design, your writing will be so hard to follow that readers either misunderstand your message or just plain give up. In this lesson, you will learn five organizational patterns, see them in action, and then imitate one of the five in your own writing.

Five Organizational Patterns

Read about these five ways to organize information in a piece of writing. Put a check mark next to each pattern that you have used before.

A. Chronological (Time) Order

You can arrange details in the order in which they happened (*first, second, then, next, later,* and so on). Autobiographical and biographical essays are almost always organized chronologically, as are science and history reports.

B. Order of Location (Spatial)

You can arrange details in the order in which they are located (*above, below, beneath,* and so on). Descriptions, observation reports, and certain explanations (such as giving directions) are organized spatially.

C. Order of Importance

You can arrange details from the most to the least important—or from the least to the most important. Persuasive essays, news stories, and most expository essays are organized by order of importance.

D. Cause and Effect

You can begin with a general statement giving the cause of a problem and then add a number of specific effects. Essays that explore or analyze problems (often based on current events) are organized in this way.

Note: The problem-and-solution method is closely related to the cause-and-effect method of organization. You state a problem and explore possible solutions.

E. Comparison

You can develop two or more subjects by showing how they are alike and how they are different.

Patrick Sebranek, Dave Kemper, Verne Meyer, *Write Source 2000* (Wilmington, MA: Great Source Education Group, Inc., 1999), p. 60

Name That Pattern!

Here are three short paragraphs, each using one of the organizational patterns you just read about. As you read each paragraph, decide which pattern the author is using. Feel free to circle any key words in each paragraph that you think are clues to the pattern. Put the letter of your choice on the line.

A Chronological Order   **D Cause and Effect**

B Order of Location   **E Comparison**

C Order of Importance

Sample 1

Because of the attack on the World Trade Center and the Pentagon, airport security has been extra tight since September 11, 2001. Beefed-up security means longer lines at ticket counters and security checkpoints before you can enter a terminal. If you are not a ticketed passenger, you can no longer say good-bye to friends and family at the gate or greet them there as they get off the plane. Some airport businesses have had to shut down because of fewer customers. It's all part of the new security program.

Organizational Pattern _____

Sample 2

When we reached the top of the mountain, the view took my breath away. Directly in front of us stretched miles of trees, rocks, and hills. Along the horizon, we could see the ocean. Straight down from where we stood was a several-hundred-foot drop-off, and at the bottom of that, a pile of rather jagged-looking rocks. Turn in any direction and the view would change.

Organizational Pattern _____

Sample 3

Weekends are supposed to be for rest and play, aren't they? Then how come I feel so tired? I got up at 6 to go out for breakfast with my dad and his friend Jon. By 8, we were on our way to my basketball tournament.

My first game was at 9, and I could still taste the pancakes and bacon. After my first game, which we won, we jumped in the car to go watch my sister, Ann, play at her basketball tournament. By noon, I was worn out.

Organizational Pattern _____

Imitating a Pattern

Choose one of the organizational patterns to create a short paragraph (six or more sentences). You'll need to choose *your own topic.* Here are some possibilities—or you can come up with any topic of your own:

- Living in your neighborhood versus living somewhere else
- Directions for what to do if you become lost
- The view from a favorite place
- How life at school changes from kindergarten to Grade 6

_____

_____

_____

_____

_____

_____

A Writer's Question

As a writer, why do you think it is important to spend some time thinking about organizational patterns and learning about some new ones? How will this help your writing?

name: _____ date: _____

The Right Tool for the Job

Would you ever pound a nail with a shovel? Brush your teeth with a broom? Sweep the deck with a toothbrush? Of course not! You would try to find the right tool for the job so that the task would be easier and the results more satisfying (and less painful). The same goes for writing. Good writers think about their topics and then select an organizational pattern that will make the message easy to understand and interesting to read.

Seven Patterns: The Right Tools to Organize Your Writing

In the previous lesson, we looked at five common organizational patterns. For this lesson, we will review those patterns and look at two more. As you read the descriptions carefully, think about any of your own writing that uses one or more of these patterns.

Remember these from Lesson 5?

A. Chronological (Time) Order—Arranging details in the order in which they happened (*first, second, then, next, later,* and so on.)

B. Order of Location (Spatial)—Arranging details according to location (*above, below, beneath,* and so on.)

C. Order of Importance—Arranging details from the most to the least important—or from the least to the most important.

D. Cause and Effect—Beginning with the cause of a problem and then explaining specific effects.

Note: The problem-and-solution method is similar to the cause-and-effect method. You state a problem and then explore possible solutions.

E. Comparison—Showing how two subjects are alike or different.

Now for two new ones . . .

F. Step-by-Step—Explaining to the reader, step-by-step, how to do something.

G. Main Idea and Support—Starting with a main idea and then framing it with supporting details to help the reader understand it better.

Match Them Up!

Carefully consider each task on the list and then select the organizational pattern that you think is the best match. While making your decision, think about the purpose of each task. What organizational approach will keep your writing *focused* and *interesting*? Write your answer, using letters A through G.

Seven Writing Tasks

1. A description of your favorite painting from the art museum field trip

Organizational Pattern _____

2. A diary of your week at Outdoor School

Organizational Pattern _____

3. An opinion paper on why the school day should be lengthened

Organizational Pattern _____

4. A campaign speech giving reasons why you should vote for a particular candidate

Organizational Pattern _____

5. A newspaper article about the mysterious vandalizing of playground balls and equipment

Organizational Pattern _____

6. An article on how snowboarding is more challenging than skiing

Organizational Pattern _____

7. An explanation of how raising the price of hot lunches will help solve a school's budget problems

Organizational Pattern _____

Share and Compare

For each of the seven writing tasks, be prepared to explain why you made the choice you did. Is it possible to have more than one "right" answer for a particular writing task?

Putting a Pattern to Use

Write a short paragraph explaining to your audience why

_____ is your favorite season. Pause for a moment before writing, and select the organizational pattern that you think will work best for your topic to keep it *focused* and *interesting* for your readers.

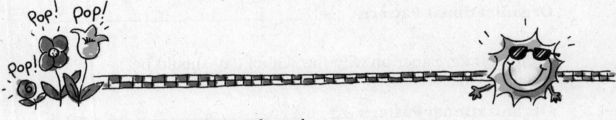

Organizational pattern I selected _____

_____

_____

_____

_____

_____

_____

A Writer's Question

Take a look at a piece of writing from your writing folder. It won't matter whether it's a rough or a final draft. What organizational pattern did you use?

_____ Did you choose the right tool for the job—or should you make a change?

name: .... date: ....

Building Bridges: Connecting Ideas

Imagine each sentence in a paragraph as an island. If the writer doesn't build "bridges" connecting one sentence island to the next, a reader may have a tough time making the mental leap. Skilled writers never leave readers stranded. They use specific words and phrases that build word bridges from one sentence or idea to the next. These word bridges, or *transitions,* make it easy for a reader to follow the writer's thoughts.

Sharing an Example: Voyage of a Summer Sun

In the passage on page 34, the author has chosen transitions to help you see what he is seeing from his canoe. There are many kinds of transitions. Those in this paragraph help show place, location, or direction. Cody (the author) wants you to connect each carefully selected image to make a complete picture in your mind.

A light breeze came from the south, bending lake reeds in the direction I wanted to go, up the west shore. Across the narrow lake, timber furred the slope. On top, snowcapped pinnacles of Rockies appeared only in the bare-rock gaps between nearer mountains. On my side of the lake, sheer sandstone cliffs leveled off to a high bench of hay fields and horse pasture. The highway rode the bench, out of sight and sound. Columbia Lake was all mine. I saw no other person, no other boat, all morning. From holes in white sandstone, blue-backed swallows dived at the canoe and veered away. Puffed clouds bunched at peaks east and west, but the sky above stayed blue and the lake took on a deep, scope green close to shore.

Robin Cody, *Voyage of a Summer Sun* (Seattle: Sasquatch Books, 1995), pp. 16–17

Transitions

Take a look now at a list of transitions and linking words. Notice how the words and phrases have been grouped into categories based on the purpose of your writing.

Words that can be used to **show location:**

above	behind	by	near	throughout
across	below	down	off	to the right
against	beneath	in back of	onto	under
along	beside	in front of	on top of	
among	between	inside	outside	
around	beyond	into	over	

Words that can be used to **show time:**

while	first	meanwhile	soon	then
after	second	today	later	next
at	third	tomorrow	afterward	as soon as
before	now	next week	immediately	when
during	until	yesterday	finally	suddenly

Words that can be used to **compare two things:**

likewise	as	while	in the same way
like	also	similarly	

Words that can be used to **contrast things** (show differences):

but	still	although	on the other hand
however	yet	otherwise	even though

Patrick Sebranek, Dave Kemper, Verne Meyer, *Write Source 2000* (Wilmington, MA: Great Source Education Group, Inc., 1999), p. 106

Some More Practice

Carefully read this short passage from *Jack on the Tracks* by
Jack Gantos. Work with a partner, using the list of transitional
words and phrases, and underline any transitions that you find.
You may find some transitional words that are not on the list.
Remember, you are looking for *any* words or phrases that build
a bridge from one sentence or thought to another. **HINT:**
Sometimes a transition comes in the middle of a sentence.

While I was thinking about the mysterious differences between boys and girls,
Mrs. Pierre turned her back toward us and faced the blackboard. Above the
alphabet letters on top of the board she had mounted a rearview mirror from a car
so she could keep her eyes on us even as she wrote, and when she did write, it was
amazing. She put a piece of chalk in each hand and stretched them out as far as
she could. Then she started writing with both hands at the same time. Her left
hand wrote normally from the beginning of the sentence to the right. Her right
hand was incredible. She started with the period of the sentence, and then with the
last letter of the last word, and continued to write completely backward from right
to left. She did this with ease, and she did it all in cursive, and she finished the
sentence exactly in the middle where her two hands met and seamlessly completed
the final word.

Jack Gantos, *Jack on the Tracks: Four Seasons of Fifth Grade* (New York: Farrar, Straus & Giroux, 2001),
p. 41

Share and Compare

Be prepared to share with your class the transitional words and
phrases you and your partner found. Your teacher will suggest
some transitional words or phrases, and you may have found
some that no one else did. It's OK to underline any you may
have missed. How did you do?

_____ We found several good transitions.

_____ We found one or two transitions, but we should have
looked harder!

_____ We did not find *any* transitions. It was hard to see how
these sentences were connected!

You Build the Bridges

Now it's your turn to build the bridges! Carefully read the passage below with a pen or pencil in your hand. If you find a section that seems to be missing a transition (a word bridge), put one in. If you find a transition that just doesn't sound right, cross out the old one and put in a better one. Use the list of transition words on page 34 to help you find just the right transitional word or words. HINT: Feel free to write sentences a little differently if it helps make your transitions smoother.

The news report said there could be snow in the morning. Then I found my boots, gloves, and hat. And I ran upstairs to tell my sisters the good news. Finally, I told my brother the good news also. He was pretty excited about the possibility of having a day off from school. On the other hand, my sisters were pretty happy about it. My mom was the only one who didn't think that a snow day would be fun. In conclusion, she would be the only one who wouldn't, therefore, get a real day off. Finally, we kept our celebration to ourselves.

A Writer's Question

Have you taken a close look lately at the kind of transitions you've been using in your own writing? Choose one piece from your folder, and read it to yourself. Add any transitions you need, and change any that are not as strong as they could be. How did you do?

_____ **I did not change anything. My transitions were VERY strong.**

_____ **I changed/added one or two new transitions.**

_____ **I made a TON of changes. Those bridges are strong now!**

name: .... date: ....

Putting It All Together

In a typical basketball practice you might spend some time doing drills: dribbling, passing, shooting free throws, and so on. Some people don't like drills because they're just practice—they're not the same as playing the game! You may feel that way about writing—practicing leads, organizational patterns, transitions, conclusions . . . "Come on!" you may be thinking, "When do we get to put this all together and just write?" Well, the answer is *now*! Here's your chance to select what goes into a paragraph, create an intriguing lead, organize the information to keep it focused and interesting, find the perfect transitions to keep all your thoughts connected, and then come up with a conclusion that wraps it all up. Ready? Let's get in the game!

Keep, Toss, and Narrow

Imagine yourself at an information grocery store with a cart labeled "My Topic." What do you want to put in your cart, and what do you want to leave on the shelf? As you read the following list of facts and details about coral snakes, put a **star** by any bit of information you want to include and an **X** right through the number of anything you want to leave out because it's too general or not interesting enough.

1. Australia has many poisonous snakes.

2. The coral snake is highly venomous, and its bite can be deadly to humans.

3. Lizards and other small snakes are the coral snake's main source of food.

4. Many people fear snakes.

5. Coral snakes are usually rather shy.

6. They spend most of their lives buried in the soil or burrowed under rocks.

7. Coral snakes are not considered aggressive.

8. Coral snakes usually have a black snout and red, yellow, black, and white bands.

9. Some snakes are considered mimics of the coral snake.

10. If you try to hold or restrain a coral snake, it will try to bite.

11. They have small heads, which makes it hard to hold them behind the head.

12. To tell the real coral snake from a mimic snake, remember this rhyme:
"Red and yellow, kill a fellow; red and black, friend of Jack."

13. Yellow-red-yellow = coral snake; red-black-red = mimic snake.

14. If threatened, the coral snake may flatten its body to look larger.

15. There are many different kinds of snakes in the world.

What's the Big Idea?

Look over the list of things you kept for your "My Topic" shopping cart. How do they go together? What is one MAIN topic? Write it here.

_____

_____

Ready to Write?

Look over your list again. What kind of pattern would fit your topic? Compare/contrast? Order of location? Cause and effect? Order of importance? Or something else? Ask yourself, "What would be the best way to organize my information to keep it focused and interesting?" You may want to look back to lessons 5 and 6 to remind yourself about various organizational patterns. Write the organizational pattern that makes sense here. _____

Off to a Good Start—The Toss-Up

A good toss-up puts the game in motion. Similarly, a lead should kick off your writing by pulling your readers in—and perhaps by giving them a hint of what is to come. Look again at your list of details. Perhaps one stands out as a good place to begin. Use it to write one possible lead here.

_____

_____

_____

_____

_____

Keep the Game Going

Don't stop the flow! Let your lead take you right into your paragraph. You do not need to use every detail you marked, but try to make your paragraph at least six sentences long. **HINT:** Use the lead you wrote above, or write a new one. Do not forget a concluding sentence that leaves your reader with something to think about. Start writing on page 40.

_____

_____

_____

_____

_____

_____

_____

_____

_____

_____

_____

_____

Share Your Paragraph

Be prepared to share your paragraph with a partner. Listen for the following features, and offer any comments that could help the writer.

- A strong lead
- A pattern that fits the topic
- Good transitions (word bridges)
- A thoughtful conclusion that wraps things up

A Writer's Question

What do you think was the organizational strength of your paragraph? Mark your strength with a check mark. Mark any area(s) you still need to work on with an X.

Lead _____

Pattern _____

Transitions _____

Conclusion _____

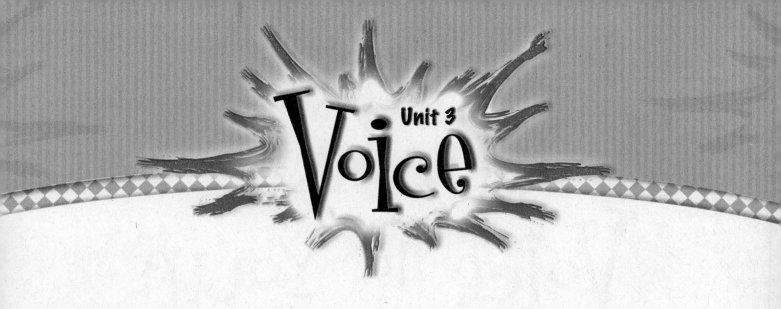

Unit 3 Voice

Writer and teacher Donald Murray once called voice the quality separating writing that is read from writing that is not read. In short, if you want people to read what you have written, you had better put some voice into it!

Maybe you're thinking, "Wait a minute! Isn't voice mostly personality on paper? How do I *learn* to have more personality?" Don't worry; the personality part of voice is already inside you. You need to learn to let it out on paper. Besides, personality is only part of the picture. As you'll discover, writers use many strategies to enhance voice, such as writing for a particular audience, researching a topic, using intriguing details, and projecting enthusiasm when writing.

In this unit you'll learn about finding and using your own voice. You will learn about

◆ listening or reading for voice

◆ identifying voice in expository writing

◆ matching voice to the purpose and the audience

◆ revising to improve voice

name: .... date: ....

Defining Voice in Your Own Words

How many different voices are there? There are singing voices, squeaky voices, deep voices, inside and outside voices, happy or sad voices, voices of authority, motherly or fatherly voices, and . . . authors' voices! Does your writing have voice? How would you know? Well, you'd need a personal definition of voice so you could recognize it. In this lesson, you'll do just that by listening to several writers' voices and deciding whether each one is likely to appeal to readers and why.

Voices on Parade

One of the best ways to define the term *voice* is to read different kinds of voices. Read each of the following passages carefully. Read them more than once, listening each time for the writer's voice. Use the scale after each passage to rate it according to the amount of voice you heard. Then, describe that writer's voice.

© Great Source. Permission is granted to copy this page.

name: .... date: ....

Voice 1

On the first day of school, Amanda's mother begged her to wear her blue dress with the pink flowers. But Amanda insisted on wearing her ladybug T-shirt that said, AMANDA FRANKENSTEIN: FRIEND OF BUGS. She carried her new magnifying glass in a special pocket of her backpack. And she wore her purple dragonfly pin for good luck.

Mrs. Scorpio, her teacher, had a dress the color of a luna moth and hair like a beehive. She led the class in a song, *"The ants go marching one by one, Hurrah! Hooray! The last stops to suck her thumb . . ."* and Amanda sang the loudest.

Megan McDonald, *Insects Are My Life* (New York: Orchard Books, 1995)

Words that describe this voice:

_____

Voice 2

It's my job to put out the recycling box and garbage can every Wednesday morning. It's also my job to put them back along the side of the house when I get home from school. I get mad sometimes because the garbage people don't put the lid back on the can carefully. Sometimes it has rolled or been blown almost two houses down. If it has been raining, the can will get water in it. If I don't pour it out, my dad will get mad. This makes me mad. All they have to do is put the lid back on and everything will be OK.

Words that describe this voice:

_____

Voice 3

I crept up on my diary. Carefully, I undid the lock with the small key I kept on a string around my neck, then slowly opened it.

"Ughhhh," I moaned. The pages were filled with squished spiders. I slammed it shut like a tiny coffin.

It wasn't the spiders that scared me. I had pressed them into the book. It was all those blank pages. For *three years* I had been trying to fill them, but I could never think of anything interesting to write. It was as if my brain stopped working if I even thought of my diary.

This didn't make any sense. Usually, I was pretty good at imagining things. When I looked at the picture of the sailboat on my wall, in my mind I could see Dad racing the Flying Dutchman yacht of his dreams. When I read a good book, like *The Feathered Serpent,* the words filled my brain with people, smells, and sounds. But when I opened my diary, my mind went blank as the paper. I felt like a moron.

Jack Gantos, *Heads or Tails: Stories from the Sixth Grade* (New York: Farrar, Straus & Giroux, 1994), p. 3

1	2	3	4	5	6
Barely any voice					Strong clear voice

Words that describe this voice:

_____

Reflection

Take a moment to think about the voices in the passages you read. Which voice do you particularly like? Which voice sounds closest to your own?

I like Voice _____.

A voice somewhat like my own is Voice _____.

Time To Define

Write your own definition of voice. Having your own definition will help you fine-tune your own voice as a writer. Before you start, take one more look at the passages and your comments. Be sure to use complete sentences.

My Definition of Voice:

_____

_____

_____

_____

Share and Compare

Get together with at least two other classmates. Take turns reading your definitions. Listen carefully to how the other writers in your group have defined voice. Do their definitions sound like yours? Did they use different words?

A similarity I heard: _____

_____

Something I hadn't thought of: _____

_____

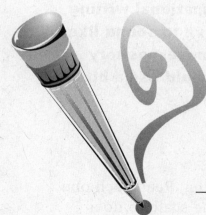

A Writer's Question

What advice would you give to someone who told you, "All those passages sounded the same to me. What's the big deal about voice?" Write what you would tell this person.

_____

_____

_____

name: .... date: ....

Voice and Expository Writing

Suppose you're writing an essay about a novel you've read or a report about the Eastern coral snake. Does that mean you suddenly abandon your voice? Not if you want anyone to read what you have written. Good expository writing has strong voice, but it's a different voice from what you hear in most fiction. A report on rats doesn't sound the same as a story about a family of rats living in a barn. Voice in expository writing comes from confidence (writers who know their topics have more voice) and the way the writer presents information. Informational writing may be loaded with facts, but it doesn't have to sound like a report. In this lesson, you will review some expository writing and work on revising a piece that could use a bit more zip.

Read, Rate, and Rank

Here are three short pieces of expository writing. Read each one carefully. Then, working with a partner, use the scale to do a quick voice rating before moving on to the next piece. When you have finished reading and rating, discuss the three samples with your partner, and rank them according to the strength of the voice in each piece.

Sample A

Coral Snakes

"Red and yellow, kill a fellow, red and black, friend of Jack." This little rhyme is a helpful way to tell the difference between a poisonous coral snake and a harmless "mimic" like the scarlet king snake. Even if your name is Matthew or Sarah, knowing the difference could save your life. Coral snakes usually have a black snout followed by a series of red, yellow, white, and black bands. The red bands are always surrounded by yellow bands, which, of course, is your signal to watch out. Not that you're likely to have an encounter with a coral snake. Coral snakes are usually pretty shy, spending most of their time burrowed under a rock or down in the soil. You'd have to try to grab or hold one down before it would try to bite. Coral snakes even have several tricks that make grabbing them as difficult as possible.

1	2	3	4	5	6
Voice? Flat and lifeless					Voice? Energetic and informative

Sample B

Australia

Australia is an island country and the only island continent. Some well-known cities are Sydney, Brisbane, Perth, and Canberra. There are many poisonous and deadly creatures in Australia. The world's ten most deadly snakes are native to Australia. There are sharks, spiders, jellyfish, crocodiles, ticks, and fish that can harm or kill you. The Great Barrier Reef is located off the coast of Australia. It is considered the world's largest living thing. Ayer's Rock is located in Australia. Its official name is Uluru, its Aboriginal name. Aborigines are the native people of Australia.

1	**2**	**3**	**4**	**5**	**6**
Voice? Flat and lifeless					Voice? Energetic and informative

Sample C

Khufu: Builder of the Great Pyramid

While the Great Pyramid of Giza, which stood 481 feet tall, is considered one of the seven wonders of the world, not much is known about the king who is responsible for it. Even though he ruled for nearly 24 years, the only thing found depicting him is a nine-inch statue. That's pretty strange for a man who built something so tall. The statue wasn't even found at Giza; it was found in a temple to the south of the Great Pyramid. Khufu's father, Senefru, also a great pyramid builder, was known as a kinder, more benevolent leader than his son. Khufu did possess, though, a great ability to organize and lead his people. Under Khufu's leadership, the pyramid was built without slave labor. Those who worked on the project did so instead of paying taxes.

1	**2**	**3**	**4**	**5**	**6**
Voice? Flat and lifeless					Voice? Energetic and informative

Ranking by Voice

Review your voice ratings for each passage before ranking them. HINT: You're not rating and ranking the topics but the voice behind the information.

Strongest Voice—Sample _____

(Consistent and interesting—I could have kept right on reading.)

Middle-of-the-Road Voice—Sample _____

(A bit inconsistent—but it had some interesting moments.)

Flat-as-a-Pancake Voice—Sample _____

(Facts without flair—thankfully, it was *short*.)

Revising for Voice

Select one of the passages that you ranked lowest in voice to revise in order to strengthen the voice. Mark your changes on the passage and begin your revision here.

_____

_____

_____

_____

_____

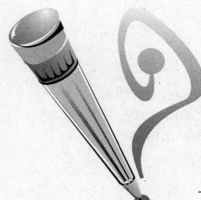

A Writer's Question

Did you have a chance to share your revised piece? What kinds of changes did you make to increase the voice?

_____

_____

name: .... date: ....

"Hello, How Are You?" or "Waz Up?"

You're at school telling friends about the loud, colorful celebration on New Year's Eve. Later in the day, you're about to share the same story with one of your teachers. Are you going to use the same words, expressions, and voice you used with your friends? You probably won't, because your *audience* is different. Audience affects voice in writing, too. In writing, it's even more important to be aware of who your audience is. On paper, there's no "you" to make facial expressions, put in sound effects, or wave your arms to emphasize a point. You have to do it all with your voice—and you have to be sure you use the right voice to reach your audience.

Sharing an Example: Saving Sweetness

This short example from the book *Saving Sweetness* by Diane Stanley shows the importance of knowing your audience. If Mrs. Sump is going to get the sheriff to do what she wants, she'd better find the right voice.

name: .... date: ....

Out in the hottest, dustiest part of town is an orphanage run by a female person nasty enough to scare night into day. She goes by the name of Mrs. Sump, though I doubt there ever was a Mr. Sump on accounta she looks like somethin' the cat drug in and the dog wouldn't eat. I heard that Mrs. Sump doesn't much like seein' the orphans restin' or havin' any fun, so she puts 'em to scrubbin' the floor with toothbrushes. Even the ittiest, bittiest orphan, little Sweetness. So one day, Sweetness hit the road.

I found out right away because Mrs. Sump came bustin' into Loopy Lil's Saloon, hollerin' like a banshee.

"Sheriff!" she yelled (that's me). "That provokin' little twerp—I mean that dear child, Sweetness, done escaped—I mean disappeared! And I'm fit to be tied, worryin' about that pore thang all pink and helpless, wanderin' lost on the plains and steppin' on scorpions and fallin' in holes and such. You gotta bring her back alive—er, I mean safe—before she runs into Coyote Pete!"

That did it. Scorpions were one thing. But Coyote Pete is as mean as an acre of rattlesnakes, and the toughest, ugliest desperado in the West.

Diane Stanley, *Saving Sweetness* (New York: Puffin Books, 1996)

Reflecting

What do you think? Did Mrs. Sump find the right voice to get her way? Write down two words that would describe her voice:

One word would be _____

Another would be _____

Identify two strategies that author Diane Stanley uses to put voice into her writing.

1. _____

2. _____

A Different Voice

Imagine that Mrs. Sump is telling a neighbor or a friend (if she had one) about Sweetness and her disappearance. What might she say about Sweetness, knowing she has a different audience? What kind of voice would she use? Imagine that you are Mrs. Sump. Write what you (as Mrs. Sump) might say to a neighbor, using a different voice from the one she used with the sheriff.

_____

_____

_____

_____

_____

Share and Compare

Share with a partner your new voice for Mrs. Sump. Was your new voice anything like your partner's? How would you describe this new voice? Write some words that come to mind.

I would describe Mrs. Sump's new voice as _____

or _____.

Writing for Two Different Audiences

In this part of the lesson, you'll flex your voice even more. You are going to write two letters, one to a friend and the other to a teacher (or your school principal). In these letters, you will tell each audience about a student who is bullying kids outside the school. Each letter needs to be at least six sentences long. Remember, voice is affected by the details you include and the words you use.

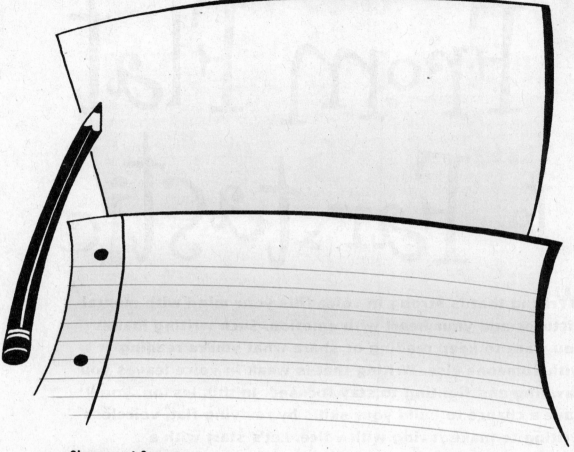

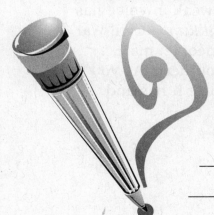

Share and Compare

Meet with a partner to share letters. To make sure that the voice in each letter is appropriate for its particular audience, don't share the greetings when you read your letters aloud. See whether your partner can tell which letter is for the teacher or principal and which letter is for the friend.

A Writer's Question

Imagine a third audience—a parent. Would the voice for this letter be just like the voice you used for the teacher? How would it be different?

_____

_____

_____

From Flat to Fantastic

Writing that is strong in voice fills your mind with mental pictures and your heart with emotion. Such writing makes you want to keep reading or share what you're reading with someone else. Writing that is weak in voice leaves you yawning and fighting to stay focused. In this lesson, you'll have a chance to build your skills by reviving flat, voiceless writing to make it ring with voice. Let's start with a comparison.

Sharing an Example: Bull Run

Writing that is strong in voice gives off its own energy. That energy might come from humor, sadness, outrage, confidence, joy, enthusiasm, or curiosity. Writing that is weak in voice has almost no energy. Here is a passage from *Bull Run,* a Civil War story told from the point of view of sixteen people: male, female, old, young, black, white, northern, southern. As you read this passage, ask yourself how much voice it has and where the voice is coming from.

Toby Boyce

I was eleven years old and desperate to kill a Yankee before the supply ran out. It seemed that all Georgia had joined except me. I knew I'd never pass for eighteen. You can't very well lie about your height. Then I heard that musicians were needed to play for the soldiers, any age at all. I hotfooted it fifteen miles to the courthouse and took my place in line. The recruiter scowled when I reached the front. "You're a knee baby yet," he said. "Go on home." I told him I meant to join the band. "And what would your instrument be?" he asked. My thinking hadn't traveled that far. "The fife," I spoke out. Which was a monstrous lie. He smiled at me and I felt limp with relief. Then he stood up and ambled out the door. Across from the courthouse a band had begun playing. We all heard the music stop of a sudden. A few minutes later the recruiter returned. He held out a fife. "Give us 'Dixie,'" he said. I felt hot all over. Everyone waited. The fife seemed to burn and writhe in my hand like the Devil's own tail.

Paul Fleischman, *Bull Run* (New York: HarperTrophy, 1993), pp. 13–14.

Get the Voice Out!

What if we tinkered with this a bit, and rewrote it, taking out most of the voice? Now it might sound like this:

I was eleven years old and wanted to join the army. Lots of other people had joined. I knew I didn't look eighteen because I was too short. Then I heard that musicians, any age at all, were needed to play for the soldiers. I went to the courthouse and got in line. The recruiter made a face at me, then told me to go home because I was too young. I told him I wanted to join the band. I lied that I could play the fife. He went to get a fife, then told me to play "Dixie." A lot of people were looking at me. I did not know if I would do a very good job since I really did not know how to play the fife.

Seeing and Feeling

You probably noticed that in removing the voice, we also had to cut a lot of words and phrases. How did that affect what you could see and feel in the passage? Compare the two samples and the mental pictures each one creates. Then compare the feelings you had as you read each sample. Feel free to look over each sample one more time before writing your responses.

In **Sample 1**

I can see _____.

I can feel _____.

In **Sample 2**

I can see _____.

I can feel _____.

Where Is the Voice Coming From?

If you are like most readers, Sample 1 creates a much clearer picture and stronger feelings for you as a reader. What specific things does author Paul Fleischman do to put voice in this passage about Toby? See whether you can come up with at least two.

   1. _____

   2. _____

From Flat to Fantastic: "Greenway Forest"

The writing on page 57 needs help. It's like music that's playing too slowly. We need to speed up the beat! First, read the piece, and underline any passages or phrases you think are flat and voiceless. Then, bring this piece to life by revising for voice.

HINT: Think about the strategies Paul Fleischman used. Use those same strategies to bring your readers into the world of the forest!

It was a pretty day as I walked along in Greenway Forest. It was a good name for the forest because everything in it was green. I wanted to be by myself so I could think about things. I sat down, and leaned against a tree. I almost fell asleep as I listened to the interesting sounds of the forest.

Then I heard a sound that got my attention. It was coming from a bush a few feet away. I couldn't figure what was making the sound. At first I thought it was one thing, then I thought it was something else.

Then something came out of the bush. It was a porcupine, chewing on something. In about a minute it was gone. I was alone again, left to enjoy myself in Greenway Forest.

Write your revision here.

I'm so bored with these stories...

_____

_____

_____

_____

_____

_____

_____

A Writer's Question

What advice about voice would you give the author of "Greenway Forest" to help him or her as a writer in the future? (Think about something important you learned, and then pass it on.)

Unit 4
Word Choice

Imagine yourself at a restaurant looking over the menu. Maybe you'll decide on the flaky broiled flounder with savory melted butter, the crunchy romaine salad, or the charbroiled burger with crispy fries. Hungry people like the freedom to choose what sounds just right at the moment. Good writers are choosy, too; they're forever seeking that perfect word that makes all the difference. That's what this unit is about: making choices.

Word choice is power. Words not only create meaning but also create moods by touching our senses. *The wind hummed in the treetops* soothes us, but *The wind wailed eerily, snaking its way through the canyon rocks* might give us the chills. Words can wake readers up *(We rocked to the music till our feet ached with throbbing blisters)* —or put them to sleep *(We had a nice time).* Yawn! As you'll see later in this unit, word choice can be overdone, too. Although one burger tastes terrific, two or three might leave you feeling a bit overstuffed. Writers want to tantalize hungry readers, but they also need to know when to quit.

In this unit, you'll find a few writers' tricks that should help you with word choice. You'll learn about

◆ using sensory language to create vivid mental pictures

◆ using synonyms and antonyms to expand understanding of a word

◆ replacing flat, colorless language with specific word choices

◆ cutting clutter from wordy passages

Lesson 13

Feeding Your Reader's Brain

name: .... date: ....

There is no way in which to understand the world without first detecting it through the radar net of our senses. "The senses feed shards of information to the brain like microscopic pieces of a jigsaw puzzle. When enough "pieces" assemble, the brain says *Cow. I see a cow.* This may happen before the whole animal is visible; the sensory "drawing" of a cow may be an outline, or half an animal, or two eyes, ears, and a nose."

Diane Ackerman, *A Natural History of the Senses* (New York: Vintage Books, 1991), p. xvii

Maybe you're saying to yourself, "Hey! How does this stuff about the brain, a puzzle, and a cow relate to writing?" Well, the connection is clearer than you might think. Here's why: *Sensory language*—words and phrases that tickle the senses of touch, sight, taste, smell, and hearing—invites readers right inside the world your words create. In this lesson, you'll learn to feed your reader's brain with sensory language.

Sharing an Example: Town Early

Author Barry Bauska seems to know this town well. As you read his description of a town waking up, be on the lookout for the sensory words (sights, sounds, feelings, smells, or tastes).

It is early morning. Not "farm early": up an hour before dawn to break the ice in the stock watering troughs. Not that early. Just "town early," with things coming slowly to life.

The service station owner moves among his pumps, unlocking each in sequence, setting out the metal signs: Full-Service, Self-Serve, Pull Ahead to Forward Pump. He puts out the garbage cans and the squeegees and water for windshields, then sets a small rack of oil cans precisely between two pumps. He surveys the ground in front of him, spies a handful of discarded lottery tickets and pull-tabs. He bends down to collect them, scans the numbers expertly for possible winners, then drops the tickets into the trash can. . . .

Somewhere in the distance a lawn mower clears its throat, nearly dies in the effort, then spurts to life. A freight train intones its way past the three or four street crossings it must negotiate. There is a crashing and banging as the cars brake to a stop, roll backwards a few yards, then clump together in a final, grinding statement.

Barry Bauska, *Town Early* (Copyright by the author) pp. 1–2

Sensory Reaction

Reread the passage with a pencil in your hand so that you can underline any sensory details you notice. Then compare your notes with the chart below. Add details that are missing from the chart.

I see	I hear	I touch	I smell
discarded lottery tickets	lawn mower	metal signs	oil and gasoline
metal signs	train	lottery tickets	cut grass
	crashing, banging	garbage can	garbage can
	grinding metal		

Creating Your Own Chart

Here's a passage from a piece of descriptive writing about a football game interrupted by a tornado. Read it carefully with your sensory radar net on full alert. Look and listen for sensations of sight, sound, smell, taste, or touch. First, underline any words or phrases that you think are examples of sensory language. Then, list each detail on the chart that follows.

The Tornado

Running down the field to the end zone, I could hear hard breathing and feel, just for a moment, the icy breath of everyone behind me. The quarterback had thrown a perfect pass, and no one was fast enough to catch me but myself.

It was cool, the fog so thick you could eat it with a spoon. The tops of the wheat stalks in the neighboring field were frozen, and when the wind rattled them, it sounded like soft chimes. Touchdown! As I celebrated by tossing the ball into the air, we all looked up to see a dangerous-looking cloud formation. The wind was spinning around, molding the wispy puffs into something dreaded here in Iowa: a funnel cloud.

We kept playing even after the icicle-like wheat was practically being uprooted by the wind. My team had scored nearly fifty points when the wind came whistling past my ears like an out-of-tune pipe organ. My friends stopped moving. The football rolled on the grass, and everyone turned to see what they knew was coming. The tornado was on the very doorstep of our field, and we ran, the mud sucking at our feet, and thin arrows of frozen wheat stinging our arms and necks.

I see	I hear	I touch	I smell

Your Turn to Write

Picture yourself, as the last writer just did, in the midst of any outdoor activity on a particularly hot, cold, or wet day. As a way of prewriting, make some notes—words and phrases—that will help shape your description:

I see _____.

I hear _____.

I touch_____.

I smell _____.

Now, put the most powerful of your sensory details together in a descriptive paragraph at least six sentences long. OR, write a short poem, if you prefer. Feed your reader's brain with sensory information.

_____

_____

_____

_____

_____

_____

A Writer's Question

Imagine, for a moment, having to write about the best day of your life. The only catch is that you can't use any sensory language—none. How hard would it be to recreate that day in your readers' minds?

name: .... date: ....

Word Graphics

The more words you have to choose from, the more powerful your writing will be. Reading is one effective way to find new words. Another way is to sit down with a dictionary or thesaurus and a pad of paper. What about having fun with words through word games and puzzles? In this lesson, we'll try combining a little bit of all three as you look for interesting words and then use a dictionary or thesaurus to create special graphics to expand your writing vocabulary.

Sharing an Example: Grandmother's Pigeon

Read the following passage from the book *Grandmother's Pigeon,* and circle two or three words you find interesting. They might be words that are new to you, words you use in your own writing or speaking, or words you'd like to know more about.

"It is impossible," said the ornithologist, adjusting her glasses, "that in your kitchen you have raised three members of an extinct species, *Ectopistes migratorius.* These are passenger pigeons. Once upon a time, these birds were so abundant that they traveled in flocks that took three days to pass overhead, 300 million birds per hour. Their nesting colonies sometimes stretched forty miles long. They seemed limitless as leaves."

Her face took on the same grim and sadly surprised look that Grandmother's pigeon usually wore.

"The lesson they teach is this—nature is both tough and fragile. Greed destroyed them. They were killed for food by the millions, and their nesting trees were burned. The last known pigeon, whose name was Martha, died in 1914 in the Cincinnati Zoo. That is, the last pigeon that we knew about! When reality at last sinks in, I shall be in shock. I shall have to sit down. Perhaps I shall sit down now, before I fall over. Have you got any tea?"

Louise Erdrich, *Grandmother's Pigeon* (New York: Hyperion Press, 1996)

Share and Compare

Share your circled words with a partner. Did you circle the same words?

The First Step: What Kind of Word Is It?

As a first step in getting to know a word, it helps to know what kind of word it is (what part of speech). You can find this information in a dictionary if you are not sure. Remember, some words can fit in more than one category, depending on how they're used. Here's a chart showing a few of the words from the passage you just read. Add your words and your partner's words to this chart (unless they're already here). Remember, get help from the dictionary if you need it.

NOUNS	VERBS	ADJECTIVES	ADVERBS
ornithologist	stretched	extinct	sadly
flocks	adjusting	grim	usually
		abundant	
		fragile	

Building a Synonym Ladder

To get to know a word very well and to build a supply of words to use in writing is to build a synonym ladder. **Synonyms** are words that mean the same or almost the same thing: *tremendous* and *huge* are examples. To build a synonym ladder, you need a key word. Start with the word *fragile.* This key word fits on the bottom rung of the synonym ladder. Now fill the top three rungs with synonyms for the word *fragile.* The word *breakable* fits here. Add two more synonyms for *fragile.* Then build a ladder for a word that you choose.

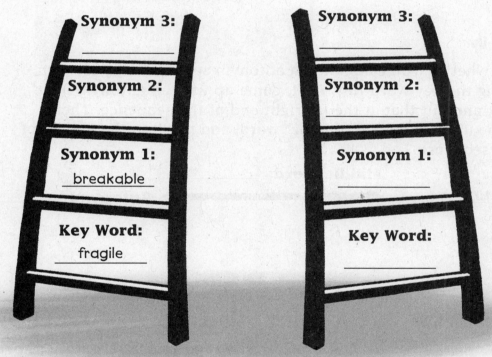

Synonym 3:
_____

Synonym 2:
_____

Synonym 1:
breakable

Key Word:
fragile

Synonym 3:
_____

Synonym 2:
_____

Synonym 1:
_____

Key Word:
_____

An Antonym Sequence

Another way to get to know a word is to think of **antonyms,** or opposites. Not every word has an antonym, though. Does the word *chair* have an antonym? How about *nonchair*? Most likely, there is no antonym for *chair.* Let's try another word from the list—*extinct.* What does the word mean? It means "no longer existing or living." A word on our list could be an antonym— *abundant,* which means "plentiful." To show antonyms, we're going to use a sequence graphic. One word goes on the left side, and its opposite goes on the right, like this:

Key Word: _extinct_  **Antonym:** _abundant_

Extinct means nonexistent. _Abundant,_ by contrast, suggests that there's no end to the supply. Is there a word whose meaning is somewhere between the two? Sure—one word is _surviving._ This word suggests that whatever we're talking about is still here (not yet extinct)—but certainly not abundant! We put the word _surviving_ right in the middle of the sequence:

Middle Word: _surviving_

Key Word: _extinct_  **Antonym:** _abundant_

Warm-Up

See whether you can build an antonym sequence of your own, using the key word _tiny._ First, come up with an antonym for _tiny,_ and put that at the far right end of the sequence. Then, come up with a good "middle" word, and put it in the middle of the sequence.

Middle Word: _____

Key Word: _tiny_ ⟵————————⟶ **Antonym:** _____

A Writer's Question

On another sheet of paper, create a short descriptive or expository paragraph, using any three of the words you used in your graphics.

name: .... date: ....

Specify to clarify

You first saw them while running to catch the bus. Now you want them—olive green convertible pants, made from nylon canvas with slash pockets in the front, two back pockets with toggle closures, and two roomy cargo side pockets. And of course, they zip off at the knee! So you venture to the store. A smiling salesperson says, "May I help you?" and (here's your big moment) you answer, "I'm looking for some pants." In an effort to be helpful, the friendly salesperson brings you denims, khakis, dress slacks, rain pants, and sweat pants, but not a single pair of olive green convertible pants, made from nylon canvas with slash pockets in the front, two back pockets with toggle closures, and two roomy cargo side pockets. Why? *Because you didn't ask for them.* Flat, general language rarely produces the results you're hoping for—whether you're shopping or writing. You won't be buying pants in this lesson, but you will get to replace flat writing with vivid, specific words that help a reader understand your meaning.

Sharing an Example: Lives of the Artists

Here's an example of writing about Leonardo da Vinci, the famous sculptor, inventor, and painter. As you read this description, underline any words or phrases that you feel are examples of specific, lively, or vivid language. (Remember—not just *pants* but *olive green convertible pants*.)

In others, Leonardo inspired devotion. He was strong, healthy, and handsome, with a carefully brushed and curled beard. His rose-colored robes were short, unlike the long robes of most men, and he was always impeccably clean in an age when most people weren't. He couldn't even stand to have paint on his fingers. He carried himself like royalty and had elegant manners. Usually he was calm, though he was known to blush when he was insulted (as by his arch-rival, Michelangelo). A welcome addition to parties, he devised clever riddles that made people roar with laughter, and he liked to play pranks that would make people scream—once he unleashed what appeared to be a dragon (actually a large lizard). He rode horses well, sang well, played the lyre well, and, of course, could invent his own musical instruments when necessary.

Kathleen Krull, *Lives of the Artists: Masterpieces, Messes (and What the Neighbors Thought)* (Orlando: Harcourt Brace & Company, 1995), p. 12

Share and Compare

Compare your notes with those of a partner, and see whether you underlined the same things. Now, pick two words or phrases that you think are the most vivid or specific, and add them to this list. We filled in the first one for you.

Leonardo da Vinci: Vivid Language

1. *impeccably clean*
2. _____
3. _____

A Short Warm-Up

What if Kathleen Krull had just written, "Leonardo da Vinci was clean, smart, and interesting"? That would have made Leonardo blend in with hundreds of other people we all know—and made Krull's writing blend in with lots of other writing, too! Anyone can write in generalities; memorable specifics take thought.

Here are three warm-up sentences for you to work on. Read each one, and circle any nonspecific, flat language you find. Then, rewrite the sentences, replacing the language you circled with specific, vivid words and phrases. Check out the example that has been done for you.

Example Sentence—

Before: The (dog went) down the (street, looking out) for (things).

After: The neighbor's black Lab, Cosmo, raced recklessly down the busy street, dodging trucks and skateboarders.

1. Before: We had a good time at the party and did fun stuff.

   After: _____.

2. Before: The flowers in the window were pretty and unusual.

   After: _____.

3. Before: The big tree moved in the wind as we looked at it.

   After: _____.

Share and Compare

With a partner, compare your new and improved sentences. Did you each circle the same words? Did your replacements, even if they were different, help create sharper pictures? Rate the power of your revisions here:

_____ Extremely powerful—I added a LOT of detail to create sharp, clear pictures.

_____ Somewhat improved—at least you can tell what each sentence is about!

_____ Hardly changed at all—my "revisions" are still too general.

Putting the Reader at the Scene

It's time to create some writing of your own. Let's try a short description of a friend or family member. Your goal is to select words and phrases that will bring this person to life on paper. Remember the description of Leonardo da Vinci? Author Kathleen Krull didn't settle for "He was fun at parties." She gave us specifics: *"Once he unleashed what appeared to be a dragon (actually a large lizard)."* Almost makes you feel as if you're at the party yourself, doesn't it? Do that for your readers, too. (Note: You may find it helpful to do some prewriting by making a word web or list of details about the person you plan to describe.) Make your description at least five sentences long.

_____ ,

_____

_____

_____

_____

Share and Compare

Take a moment now to read your description carefully. Be on the lookout for flavorless words like *nice, good, pretty, fun,* and so on. (The duller the words, the heavier your readers' eyelids get.) If your words aren't creating a clear picture, pitch them! Add detail, verve, life, color, spice, zest, gusto, zing, pizzazz— whatever it takes to awaken a snoozing reader.

A Writer's Question

When you turn flat, dull language into vivid and lively language, you have certainly improved your word choice. But what are some *other* traits that are likely to improve at the same time?

Cut the clutter!

There's a reason STOP signs have only one word on them. STOP is the *only* word needed. It gets the job done, quickly and precisely. Imagine if the sign were filled with this message: "You are approaching a street containing cars moving swiftly in either direction. Please, decrease the speed of your vehicle gradually until it comes to a full and complete stop at the white line." Whew! That's a mouthful—and a sign-ful. Good word choice is about choosing the right word for the job, not tossing every word you can think of at your victim—uh, reader—till he or she shouts, "I *get* it already!" Unneeded words just clutter your writing.

Sharing an Example

Extra words pile up clutter, which the reader has to sift through to get to the main idea. Readers who have to work that hard usually give up. Read the following piece to decide whether this writer used the right number of words or too many. Mark your response under "My Thoughts."

I walked down the aisle of the airplane, between the rows of seats, and found the seat that had been assigned to me when I checked in at the ticket counter. The plane was almost full—not totally full, but very close. There were many people on the plane, including men, women, older people, younger people, children, families, and people traveling alone. All kinds of people. I hoped that whoever was assigned the seat next to the seat I was assigned would be a quiet person and not interested in talking the whole way to Oakland. I liked it better when I could sit next to someone who didn't like to talk instead of sitting next to people who always talked. If I could just read my book and listen to my music, I would be happy. Reading my book and listening to my music helps me to relax and not worry about flying. I get too nervous and worried about flying if I can't read and listen to music, so it helps to sit near someone quiet.

My Thoughts

How would you rate this piece of writing?

_____ I'd say it's about right—in fact, the writer could say even more about why it's good to sit near a quiet person.

_____ It's a bit wordy, but that helps the reader get the message.

_____ This is way too wordy—good grief, cut the clutter!

Work with a partner to read the passage again. (Hint: Reading the passage aloud can be helpful.) Cross out any unnecessary words, phrases, or sentences. Revise to make every word count! Feel free to change the wording slightly to make your final revision read smoothly. When you think you are finished, read your revised version aloud again to make sure that you cut everything that needed to go.

Let's Compare

Compare this revised paragraph with yours. Does your paragraph look similar to this one? Did you and your partner cross out more unnecessary words? Fewer words?

I walked down the aisle of the airplane and sat in my seat. The plane was almost filled with passengers of all ages. I hoped that whoever was sitting next to me would be a quiet person. If I could just read my book and listen to my music, I would be happy and relaxed. Otherwise, I'd be nervous about flying.

Share and Compare

Let's compare revisions. After a close look, put a check next to the sentence that best describes the comparisons. (It's okay if they aren't exactly the same.)

_____ We cut even more. Ours is really short.

_____ We cut out about the same.

_____ We cut fewer words but still like our paragraph.

_____ We cut fewer words but decided next time we would cut more!

Cleaning Out the Clutter

Here's another chance to remove some clutter. As you read the following example, cross out any unnecessary words. Then rewrite the paragraph in its cleaner, shorter form. Remember the STOP sign, and make each word count. (Hint: Remember that you should feel free to change the punctuation or structure of the sentences so that your final revision reads smoothly.)

When I woke up, I looked out the big front window that is on the front of our house. It's a good, large window that's great for looking out. Just as I had thought, and anticipated, it was raining, really raining hard. It was coming down fast, all right, making everything soaking wet. I guess I should have been happy and not sad, because today's rain made it a record for something like thirty consecutive rainy days in a row for our area. Today was, I think, something like, around thirty-five days in a row where it had rained. Thirty-five days of rain is a lot of rain! The local news stations would be talking about this all day and send reporters who work for them out into different parts of town to film the rain for their reports about the rainy day record. There's nothing to be happy about or celebrate or have a party for. This is winter. The news should be about why it hasn't snowed this winter.

Share and Compare

Were you able to clean up the clutter? Share your revised paragraph with a partner. What kinds of changes did you each make? Was one revision shorter than the other? Was one stronger than the other? Discuss how you each decided what clutter to remove.

name: .... date: ....

SOME GRUESOME FEARFUL WISE wonderful that GREAT is

A Writer's Question

A writer—let's call her Wanda Wordy—has a lot of trouble keeping her writing concise. It's as if her pencil has a will of its own! Offer poor Wanda three tips to keep clutter from overcoming her.

1. _____

2. _____

3. _____

Sentence Fluency

Fluent writing is rhythmic and easy on the ear, much like a good piece of music. If you've ever listened to a song with jarring rhythm or lyrics that seemed to repeat, then you know how unpleasant or monotonous it can be. The songwriter's message is lost on you if you turn off the radio every time that song comes on. A good song, though, is all but irresistible. You may find yourself tapping your feet, drumming your fingers, or humming along. Musical writing has a magic all its own.

In this unit, you'll look at some strategies that can help make every piece of writing you create more musical. You'll learn about

◆ varying sentence lengths

◆ rewriting run-on sentences

◆ revising to make sentences more fluent

◆ analyzing a passage for fluency

name: .... date: ....

Short, Long, and In-between

Remember the old sandbox days, packing a bucket tight with sand and tipping it over to create a mountain? If you poured water on top of your creation, the water rolled down the sides, but not always *straight* down. Sometimes it twisted and turned, going faster or slower, depending on bumps in the sand. Sometimes it would flow uninterrupted for a bit, make a quick turn, then settle into a long stretch again. Strong, fluent writing does the same thing. It flows from beginning to end, but not always in a straight line and not always at the same speed. The twists and turns of the writer's ideas help create the flow. In this lesson, you will learn to vary sentence length to create some twists and turns that keep readers surprised and interested.

Sharing an Example: Notes From a Liar and Her Dog

Let's follow the flow in this passage by Gennifer Choldenko. It's about a girl named Ant (Antonia), her dog Pistachio, and her friend Harrison. Read it through once just to get a feel for it. Then read it again carefully, noticing the length of the sentences. You don't have to count the words; just ask yourself as you go, "Medium? Short? Long?"

The Emersons have a funny house. On the outside it looks like a farmhouse and a big old barn, only there isn't any cropland. Just a yard with a palm tree. On the inside, it's filled with carpet pieces from Harrison's Aunt Sue's carpet store. There isn't much in the way of furniture, though, unless you count the beanbag chairs. They are everywhere. At the Emersons they either don't have something or they have it in quantity, like there's never any scissors, but Harrison and I counted eleven vegetable peelers one day.

Gennifer Choldenko, *Notes From a Liar and Her Dog* (New York: G.P. Putnam's Sons, 2001), p. 105

Your Response

What did you think about the fluency of this passage? How is it affected by the length of each sentence? If you're not sure, try reading the passage aloud to get a better feel for the fluency.

_____ Not very fluent—no variety in sentence length whatsoever.

_____ A little fluent—some variety, but most sentences were about the same length.

_____ Very fluent—good variety in sentence length!

Seeing the Numbers

Actually, no two sentences in that passage were the same length. We're hoping you noticed how that gave the passage a strong and interesting flow. Let's look at the numbers as a way of backing up a strong rating:

Number of Sentences in Passage: **7**

Number of Words in Each Sentence: **6, 18, 7, 14, 15, 3, 29**

If you read this series of numbers aloud like words, it emphasizes the variety. The first sentence is the topic sentence, or the "What's it going to be all about?" sentence. Wherever this sentence appears, it must be clear and to the point—short to medium in length. The author then supplies some details about this "funny house" in sentences that vary in length from 3 words to 29 words. (Did you know there was *that* much variety?) By the end of the paragraph, we have a clear mental picture of the Emersons' house, and we've laughed about all those vegetable peelers. The author used short sentences to make some details stand out and used variety to keep her readers' attention. That's the power of twists and turns.

Your Turn to Crunch the Numbers

Read the next example aloud to yourself (quietly), asking yourself how sentence length affects fluency. Think about how it sounds and feels as you read it.

It almost never snows here. Our winters are all about rain. I have to carry an umbrella. My backpack is always soaking wet. My sled never gets used. I've built a snowman only once. That was at my grandparent's house. They live in Washington. They had snow every day. Besides the snowman, I built a fort. I went sledding in their pasture. I was cold sometimes, but not wet. That's what winter should be like. Instead, I get rain and mud. Making a mudman isn't much fun.

Did you enjoy reading this one aloud? How did the passage sound when you read it aloud? Lots of interesting twists and turns? Choppy and repetitive? Same old rhythm with every line? Before you pass judgment, crunch the numbers. As before, count the number of sentences. Then count the number of words in each sentence. The first sentence has been counted for you. (You might not need every space.)

Number of sentences _____ (How much room for variety in length does this give you?)

Number of words in each sentence: __5__ _____ _____ _____

_____ _____ _____ _____ _____ _____ _____ _____ _____ _____

Now check your totals with a partner. Read the totals aloud to your partner, just as if you were reading words. How does it sound? Do seeing the numbers and hearing them read aloud confirm your thoughts about the fluency of this writing? What can you do to improve the flow? Write down two revision strategies to improve fluency in this passage. Think about strategies you may have practiced before, such as sentence combining.

#1 _____

#2 _____

Revising for Variety

Read the piece on page 78 one more time. Your goal is to vary the length of the sentences, and you can use any strategy that will help you. When you're done, the writing should have a stronger sense of flow and rhythm and should be easier to read aloud. Mark the text first; then write your revised version here.

A Writer's Question

Look back at your revised paragraph. Count the words in your longest and shortest sentences. Write the numbers here: Longest _____ Shortest _____. What strategies did you use to make the piece more fluent?

_____

_____

_____

name: .... date: ....

Catching Up with Run-on Sentences

You've probably heard the old story *The Gingerbread Man,* in which the runaway gingerbread man challenges everyone by shouting, "Run, run, run just as fast as you can. You can't catch me—I'm the Gingerbread Man!" But have you ever heard the story about the Run-on Sentence? You know, the one in which words get together to form a sentence, and more and more keep joining the line? The sentence screams, "Pile on those words just as fast as you can! You can't top me—I'm the *Run-on Sentence,* man!" Run-on sentences are a menace to fluency, running poor readers ragged.

Knowing A from B

Run-ons fall into two common types. **Type A** run-ons are two or more complete sentences joined together with no capital letters or periods to separate them: *George is my friend he is tall.* Type A's are relatively easy to mend. Just add a capital letter at the beginning of the second sentence and a period (or question mark or exclamation point) at the end of the first: *George is my friend. He is tall.*

Type B run-ons are a little tougher to control. They may be a mix of complete thoughts and partial ideas slapped together with connecting words (conjunctions)—*and, then, so, but, and so, and then,* and *so then.* A Type B run-on might read like this: *We left on our trip and it was a sunny day but my brother didn't feel like going and so he stayed home with my grandmother so then the rest of us left without him but we had fun anyway.*

Sharing an Example: Dave at Night

Here's a short passage from Gail Carson Levine's book, *Dave at Night.* Dave is describing his first day at an orphanage. We'll look at this passage in three different forms. We've changed the first two to help you see run-on problems in action. The third version is, of course, the author's original.

Type A Run-ons: *Missing Ending Punctuation and Capital Letters*

Mr. Meltzer stopped in front of a door and opened it while holding on to me inside was a nurse's office with a scale and a cot and the nurse's desk, which had a telephone on it the nurse said hello and smiled like there was something to smile about she weighed me, listened to my heart, and looked in my ears when she riffled through my hair for lice, she said, "I wish I had curls like yours"

Close Up

Did you hear more than one sentence? Did you see places where punctuation or capital letters were missing? Time to revise. Drop a period in each place you hear or see a sentence ending, and insert a capital letter where you hear or see the start of a new sentence.

Type B Run-ons: Extra connecting words (conjunctions)

Mr. Meltzer stopped in front of a door and opened it while holding on to me **and** inside was a nurse's office with a scale and a cot and the nurse's desk, which had a telephone on it **so** the nurse said hello and smiled like there was something to smile about **and then** she weighed me, listened to my heart, and looked in my ears **but** when she riffled through my hair for lice, she said, "I wish I had curls like yours"

Close Up

Did you hear too many connecting words? Did you see places where you knew one idea had ended but the writer kept going? To revise this passage, try replacing each boldfaced connecting word with a period and then capitalizing the first letter of the next word.

Gail Carson Levine's Version—No Run-ons!

Mr. Meltzer stopped in front of a door and opened it while holding on to me. Inside was a nurse's office with a scale and a cot and the nurse's desk, which had a telephone on it. **T**he nurse said hello and smiled like there was something to smile about. **S**he weighed me, listened to my heart, and looked in my ears. **W**hen she riffled through my hair for lice, she said, "I wish I had curls like yours."

Gail Carson Levine, *Dave at Night* (New York: HarperCollins Children's Books, 1999), p. 30

The author's version contains five separate sentences. Does that match what you came up with in your revisions? Read this final version aloud. How does it sound to you?

_____ Highly fluent—very easy to read.

_____ OK—but it could still use some smoothing out.

_____ Not very fluent at all—tough to read aloud!

Stop the Runaway Run-on

Here are two chances to lasso a runaway run-on. Study each piece to determine whether it's a Type A, Type B, or a blend of the two. Mark each text to show your revisions.

Runaway Sentence #1

The sun was out for the first time in ages and my brother and I were dying to play with the new lacrosse sticks we had bought with our own money so then we quickly gathered all our equipment, got on our bikes and rode down to the school but there were dozens of people there with their dogs playing Frisbee so we decided to try a narrow strip of grass behind the playground and then the ground was so muddy there, however, that we just decided to go back home.

Runaway Sentence #2

It was my job to walk the neighbors' dog whenever they decided to go away for the weekend they paid me five dollars for each day I had to walk their dog, Doony, twice each day and then I also had to make sure she had food and water if she even heard me rattling her leash, she would start to bark and jump even if she didn't hear the leash, I could make her bark by saying the word "walk" as if it were a question it was really a pretty easy and fun job.

A Writer's Question

What can you do as a writer to head off those run-ons at the pass? In other words, how can you avoid letting the sentences get out of control in the first place?

name: .... date: ....

From First to Last in Fluency

One of the joys of discovering rhythmic, fluent writing is reading it aloud. The smooth phrasing, the perfect pacing, and the variety all add up to an easy, pleasurable experience. As we have suggested before, to judge the fluency of a piece of writing, you need to read it aloud. Hearing is believing.

Rate the Writing First to Last

Assessing fluency in the work of other writers is an important step in creating consistently fluent writing of your own. Here are three passages to read and rate for fluency. Work with a partner, and take turns reading each passage aloud. This will give you a chance to judge each sample as a listener and as a reader.

Sample A

I'm the kind of person who likes to spend time roughing it in the woods. I'm not talking about the kind of camping a lot of people do. You know what I'm talking about. You drive your car into one of those busy campgrounds. You pull into a paved campsite with a wooden picnic table and a metal grate over the fire pit. You can't really call this camping when there is an outlet for electricity right next to the table. There isn't any hiking involved. There's only about a five-foot walk from the car to the spot where your tent will go. And the place is crawling with people who make noise all night. Roughing it? I don't think so.

Sample B

I love to go real camping and hiking in the woods. You get to use so many different skills, like reading a map, building a fire, using a compass, and purifying water. Carrying a cool pocketknife, too. And choosing the right camping spot. Watch out for wild animals! I really love all the equipment. I love packing. I love being ready for anything. Rain can be bad though. If your sleeping bag gets wet, that's bad, too. Or your food. Knowing how to survive is the best. In the woods.

Sample C

I wouldn't exactly call myself a mountain man or anything, but I love to hike and camp in the woods. You know, real backpacking. Now, don't get me wrong. I'm not an outdoor snob or anything. It's just that driving a big RV (recreational vehicle) loaded down with all the comforts of home, including television, is nothing close to my idea of camping. You haven't earned the right to call it camping if all you have to do is drive in, connect all the hook-ups, set up the lawn chairs, and get a cold drink from the refrigerator. As for me, I want to rough it.

Fluency Rankings

Now that you've heard each piece read aloud twice, match the letter of the sample to the description that fits it best:

_____ Smooth, varied, and fluent. Easy and pleasurable to read aloud.

_____ OK, but a bit inconsistent—some smooth passages, some rough spots.

_____ Pretty hard to find the rhythm—choppy and awkward with too many sentences similar in length.

Share and Compare

Check to see how your partner rated the three pieces. Did you agree? Do you feel confident about your ratings? (**TIP:** If either of you is unsure, read the passage aloud one more time.)

Time to Revise

Read the following piece of writing aloud carefully, and ask yourself, "How can I make this piece more fluent?" Mark the copy with any reminders you need; then use the writing space provided to write out your revision. (**HINT:** Feel free to cross out words, eliminate repetition, rewrite sentences, or add words and details.)

I was standing there in the bright, hot sun. The bright, hot sun was making me squint and shield my eyes I didn't want to shield my eyes I wanted to look through my binoculars. There were birds all around and some might even be bald eagles and I looked away from the bright, hot sun, because my eyes needed a rest and I wanted to see a bald eagle so that I could tell my friends that I had spotted a bald eagle, which is an endangered species. When I looked back into the binoculars, I saw some birds flying over the lake. They were flying low. They were flying over the water. They could be fishing. Then I saw its white head just before it dropped close to the water. The bald eagle dropped down close to the water for a moment so then he caught a fish and I was looking at a bald eagle carrying a fish. The symbol of our country. And I watched it.

name: .... date: ....

_____

_____

_____

_____

_____

_____

_____

_____

_____

_____

Share and Compare

Read your revised piece once out loud, listening for smooth, flowing sentences. Meet with a partner to share your revised paragraphs. Compare your revisions. What kinds of changes did you each make? Did you each meet the goal of improving the fluency of the writing?

A Writer's Question

How does reading a piece of writing out loud help you rate it for fluency?

name: ....   date: ....

What Makes It Flow?

Think back to the time when you couldn't ride a bike, swim, jump rope, or make toast without burning it. Mastering any skill takes trial-and-error practice, plus one other important thing: You need to see someone do it. Seeing someone else riding a bike or swimming helps you get a visual sense of what it's supposed to look like. Writing is like that, too. Unfortunately, most of us don't get an opportunity to peek over the shoulder of a favorite author as he or she writes, but we can pick up a book. For this lesson, you will need a good book. It could be an old favorite, a new favorite, one you just finished, or one you're still reading. You'll need to have the book in your hands before you go on. Go get it now!

Sharing an Example: In a Dark Wood

Here's a short passage from the very beginning of the book we chose to share, *In a Dark Wood,* by Michael Cadnum. The book is filled with fluent, rhythmic sentences, linked together into smooth, flowing paragraphs. What makes the writing fluent?

The forest was quiet. Everything that was about to happen was far away, through the trees.

Geoffrey stood still, staring straight ahead, although he could see nothing but trembling patches of sunlight on the fallen leaves. A forest was like night. It was a different world, and everything a man was afraid of lived there, afraid of nothing.

The boar spear was a long, heavy weapon, and this particular spear had never been used before. Its head was slender and very sharp, and the cross-piece midway down the shaft was gleaming black. Geoffrey found a new grip on the spear, the iron cold where he had not touched it, and the horns of the beaters, and their cries, filtered through the trees, bright curls of sounds, like shavings on a goldsmith's bench.

Between them and where he stood was the most dangerous kind of beast. It could feel no pain. Its eyes were fire pricks. It weighed more than three men.

Michael Cadnum, *In a Dark Wood* (New York: Puffin Books, 1998), pp. 1–2

Breaking Fluency Down

This author knows how to use fluency to create anticipation. Would you agree? Could you feel the tension? How did the author create this rhythm? There is no pat answer or formula, but we can try to break the passage down into its important elements—sentence length, sentence beginnings, transitions, paragraph length, use of fragments or run-ons for style, and so on. See how this passage breaks out.

Number of Sentences	12
Number of Words in Each Sentence	4, 12, 20, 5, 17, 17, 18, 40, 13, 5, 5, 6
Number of Sentences with Internal Punctuation	6
Number of Paragraphs	4
Number of Sentences in Each Paragraph	2, 3, 3, 4

First Word of Each Sentence	The, Everything, Geoffrey, A, It, The, Its, Geoffrey, Between, It, Its, It
Transition or Linking Words Used	although, but, like, and, before, between
Sentence Fragments or Run-ons Used for Style	none used

Discovering Fluency

Now it's time to open that book you selected. Find a passage that you think is a strong example of fluency. Your passage needs to be about eight to ten sentences long. Read the passage aloud to make sure it has the flow you want. When you think you've found a passage that shows great fluency, write down the title of the book, the author, and the page number(s) where you found your passage.

Book Title: _____

Author: _____

Page number(s): _____

Now begin an analysis of your passage to find out what makes it flow.

Number of Sentences	
Number of Words in Each Sentence	
Number of Sentences with Internal Punctuation	
Number of Paragraphs	
Number of Sentences in Each Paragraph	

First Word of Each Sentence	
Transition or Linking Words* Used	
Sentence Fragments or Run-ons Used for Style	
Other elements I noticed	

*See the list of Transition or Linking Words found in Lesson 7, pages 34.

Summing Up Your Analysis

Look carefully at your analysis. What did the author do to create fluent writing? Use the clues you found to sum up this particular writer's strengths in fluency. Here's a sample summary based on the *In a Dark Wood* passage you read earlier. We used our chart to create it.

Summary of passage from In a Dark Wood: The author varies his sentence length a lot—from four to forty words! The variety in sentence beginnings is impressive, too; only a few begin the same way, and sometimes repetition can be effective if it makes a point. The author repeats the word "It" to help create a mysterious feeling. We do not really know what sort of beast is hiding in the woods. In addition, the author uses linking words to connect ideas.

Ready to try a summary of your own? Look over the passage you selected and the chart you created based on that passage. Then, write your own short summary here.

My summary: _____

_____

_____

_____

_____

A Writer's Question

Did your partner's passage have the same kind of rhythm as the one you chose, or was it very different? Can two fluent passages have very different sounds? Why?

Unit 6

[ConVentions]

Ever set out to do a job—mowing the lawn, raking the yard, washing the car, or vacuuming the house—and find you didn't have the right tools for the job? Without your lawn mower, rake, sponge, or vacuum, you're not likely to make much progress. Editing takes tools, too. You're probably thinking, "Well, sure—a pencil, an eraser . . ." Absolutely. Those things are a good start, but editors need much more. Real-life editors need sharp eyes and ears to help them spot errors. Knowledge of the editor's symbols (a type of editor's code) is also extremely useful. Do you have a personalized checklist that reminds you which errors are especially troublesome for you? If not, you might want to add one of those to your toolbox, too. Then, of course, it never hurts to have a dictionary and good handbook nearby so that if you're unsure about spelling or punctuation, you can look it up.

In this unit, you'll prepare for the job of editing. You'll learn about

◆ revising and editing

◆ using editor's symbols

◆ seeing and hearing errors

◆ making your own editing checklist

name: _____   date: _____

Revising, Editing, or "Revisediting"?

Would it make sense to combine walking and swimming and call them *swalking?* How about mowing and raking? Could they become *moking?* No, probably not. When it comes to writing, many young writers make the mistake of thinking that since revising and editing are related, they must be the very same thing—*revisediting,* perhaps. Bet you know better, right? You understand that revising and editing are two distinct parts of the writing process, involving different ways of thinking and different strategies. In this lesson, you'll have a chance to show what you know.

Moving Toward a Definition

Look carefully at the **Before** and **After** examples that follow. Use your experiences as a writer, your writer's common sense, and your writer's gut feeling. In each example, the writer has made some changes. Your job is to decide what kinds of changes were made and then decide whether the writer was revising or editing.

Sample 1

Before: I put the mower away. I mow the front lawn. I get the mower out. I am careful with the cord. I mow in horizontal lines. I mow in diagonal lines. I sweep up the sidewalk and driveway.

After: When it's time to mow the lawn, I carefully roll the electric mower out from the back of the garage. I first mow back and forth in horizontal lines and then diagonally. My dad likes the crisp pattern of lines. I have to be very careful the whole time I'm mowing so I don't run over the mower's cord. When I'm finished mowing, and the lawn mower is tucked away, I sweep both the sidewalk and the driveway. My dad says the job isn't done until the cleanup is done.

What happened? What kinds of changes did the writer make? Take a close look at each version, then list a few of the changes you noticed here:

_____

_____

_____

_____

_____

Now, decide whether the writer was revising or editing. Circle your choice.

Revising   **Editing**

Sample 2

Before: when it's time to mow the lown, I carefully roll the electric mower out from the back of the garage i first mow back and fourth in horizontal lines and then diagonally. My dad likes the crisp pattern of lines. I have to be very carful the whole time Im mowing so I dont run over the Mower's cord. When I'm finished mowing, and the lawn mower is tucked away, I sweep both the sidewalk and the driveway? my Dad says the job isn't done until the cleanup is dun.

After: When it's time to mow the lawn, I carefully roll the electric mower out from the back of the garage. I first mow back and forth in horizontal lines then diagonally. My dad likes the crisp pattern of lines. I have to be very careful the whole time I'm mowing so I don't run over the mower's cord. When I'm finished mowing, and the lawn mower is tucked away, I sweep both the sidewalk and the driveway. My dad says the job isn't done until the cleanup is done.

What happened? What kinds of changes did this writer make? Take a close look at each version, and then list a few of the changes you noticed here:

_____

_____

_____

_____

_____

Now, decide whether the writer was revising or editing. Circle your choice.

Revising   **Editing**

Share and Compare

With a partner, share the kinds of changes you noticed in each of the **Before** and **After** examples. Did you agree about whether the writer was **revising** or **editing?** It's OK to change your mind *if your partner has the evidence to convince you!*

Revising or Editing?

Read carefully each example of what a writer might do and decide whether you think the activity describes revising or editing. Circle your choice.

1. Adding some descriptive details to create a clearer picture for the reader.

   Revising   **Editing**

2. Inserting a comma to separate the city and state.

   Revising   **Editing**

3. Moving two paragraphs to create a more logical flow in a story.

   Revising   **Editing**

4. Varying the beginnings of the sentences in a paragraph to create better fluency.

   Revising   **Editing**

5. Correcting the spelling of "sincerely" in the closing of a letter.

   Revising   **Editing**

Time to Define

Now it's time to define each term. Your definitions should be different and should clearly show that you understand what writers do when they revise and when they edit.

Revising is _____.

Editing is _____.

A Writer's Question

Sometimes using an analogy, or comparison, is a great way to show understanding of two different but related ideas. See whether you can finish this analogy:

If revision is like changing your entire outfit minutes before going to a party, then editing is like: _____.

The Editor's Code

In secret agent/spy movies, the agents often use a secret code to communicate. It could be a combination of letters, numbers, or symbols, or even a pattern of colors. The whole point is to keep the "other side" from understanding the message. Editors often use a code, too, but unlike spies, they do not try to keep their code secret. The editor, the writer, or anyone looking at the paper should be able to understand the message. How about you? Have you cracked the editor's code? If not, stand by—we're about to let you in on ten important symbols that will tell you exactly what the editor's message is.

The Power of Ten

In this lesson, you'll get reacquainted with eight symbols you have probably worked with before and meet two new symbols you can add to your repertoire. Don't panic if all ten symbols are new, or if the whole idea of using editor's symbols is new to you! You can refer to the chart during the exercises. The idea is to create fast, meaningful writer-to-editor communication by choosing and using the symbol that matches the message.

Editor's Symbols

Mark	Meaning	Use
1.	Delete (Take it out.)	My dog is the my friend.
2. ∧	Add a word.	Pizza is favorite food. (my)
3. ≡	Capitalize this letter.	I live in portland.
4. /	Make this a lowercase letter.	My sister is Older than I am.
5. ⊙	Add a period.	I am leaving on Tuesday⊙
6. ∧,	Add a comma.	I ate juice, toast, and cereal.
7. ˇ'	Add an apostrophe.	The neighbors dog bit me.
8. ˇˇ	Add quotation marks.	I'm having a blast, he shouted.
9. ¶	Start a new paragraph.	"Wild dogs!" yelled Joe. "Should we run?" Jacob asked.
10. (Run in)	No new paragraph; sentences should run together.	Skateboarding is more fun (Run in) than walking. It's even more fun than flying.

Warming Up to the Code

When you know and use editors' symbols, it keeps you involved at the polishing stage just as you are involved at every step of the writing process. The symbols provide clear, concise messages that help the editor (that usually means you!) go straight to work. Here are some warm-up exercises for you. "Read" the editor's symbols, crack the code, and then write down what the symbols are telling the editor to do. Remember, it's OK to refer to the chart of symbols any time you need a refresher.

please, stop bothering me!" Hannah yelled. "what are you going

to do, tell Dad" asked her sister.

The coded message tells the writer or editor to _____

_____

_____

i think rainy ~~days~~ days are the best.

When it rains, I like to go out and jump in puddles plug up the

street drain and float sticks in front of the neighbors House

The coded message tells the writer or editor to _____

_____

_____

Ill mow the **lawn** tomorrow, if It doesnt rain.

The coded message tells the writer or editor to _____

_____

_____

Using the Code to Send a Message

You should be warmed up now, with your editor's eye and ear
ready to work. Here's a piece of writing in desperate need of
editing. It's your turn to use the symbols,
the editor's code, to send the writer a
message about what needs to be done.
You only need to put in the symbols;
you don't need to rewrite the
paragraph. Refer to the chart
whenever you're not sure which
symbol to use.

Olympic Skating

one of my favorite events in in the olympics is speed skating.

In my mind it is so much better figure skating which is my sisters favorite event My Sister and I were arguing about which was better. She said, Who cares about how fast you go! Besides, i like the music and the the Costumes." "Music and costumes! I yelled. "Speed skaters go so fast they have to wear helmets." She just doesnt get it. With the helmets the long-bladed skates the aerodynamic suits, and the speed, what could be better?

I guess we'll have to agree to disagree about the skating, or see whether we can can make brother-sister arguing an olympic event.

Code Check

Get together with a partner to check your work. Did you spot the same errors? Did you code each error with the same symbol? Did you feel frustrated that the writer had made so many errors? Check to make sure that you caught all the errors and marked them with the right symbols.

A Writer's Question

Look carefully at the paragraph you just worked on. Did the writer's errors slow your reading down? What impact will a corrected version have on the writer's ideas?

Eyes, Ears, Rules, and Tools

name: .... date: ....

What does it take to be an editor? A diploma from editing school? A badge? A cool hat? Actually, it takes a keen eye for spotting errors, a properly tuned ear for those errors that you can hear, knowledge of some basic rules of language (and some common sense), and a set of editing symbols (tools) for communicating with the writer. Of course, you'll need a pencil as well. Whether you're editing your own work or the work of another writer, your goal each time is to get more comfortable with the job, more familiar with the symbols, a little faster with your pencil, and even more tuned in with your eyes and ears. As you become more aware of the kinds of errors you tend to make, editing your own work will take less time; eventually, you may get so fast you'll start catching yourself even before you make a mistake.

Getting Focused

Read each sentence in the example aloud to yourself. (Remember, reading aloud is the best way to really hear the writer's language, including the mistakes.) Use the editing symbols from the chart on page 98 to mark the mistakes you spot.

I'm from Wisconsin, where there are are real winters with lots of snow ice and below-zero temperatures when I moved to oregon, I had to laugh the first time it snowed.

I wouldnt even have called it snow but everyone around here all excited. All the local news people put on these Parkas with their channel number and logo. Stay tuned to News 5 for all the traffic and weather updates as we cover *Winter Storm 2002*," the announcer said very seriously. "Winter storm! Ha!" my brother and I yelled back at the the TV. These people don't know what winter storm really is.

Number of errors I spotted: _____
Number of different editor's symbols I used: _____

A Job for the Editor

Read the passage aloud to yourself. As you read, pencil in hand, mark any errors you find with the proper editing symbols.

About a Year ago, a new high school was was built in neighborhood. It's within walking distance of my house, which is good. The problem is all the extra traffic that now comes through our neighborhood.

There are a lot more cars than there used to be, and most of them are driven by younger drivers. This makes my parents nervous. It seems as if there are more cars going too fast and fewer cars actually stopping at the intersection near our house. "Mina, my father said to me last night, "youve got to be extra careful crossing the street and riding your bike. "Trust me," i told him, "I want to live to be a seventh grader."

The neighbors got together at the high school for a meeting with people from the city the police department and from the school. they came up up with a plan to put in speed bumps to slow down the. Now, all we have to do is get everyone in the neighborhood to agree to the plan

Number of errors I spotted: _____

A Writer's Question

Describe how confident you feel as an editor.

_____

_____

Lesson 24

A Personalized Checklist

A good car is still a good car, even when it's covered with dust and grime. A little wax and polish surely make a difference, though. Writers know that editing is like putting wax and polish on their ideas. A writer may have the most creative idea in the world, but if it's buried under conventional errors, it isn't very likely to catch a reader's eye. If you want your ideas to be noticed, you need the wax and polish of good editing. One tool that can make your editing much stronger is a personalized checklist. How do you go about creating one? First, pay close attention to the mistakes you make most often. Be honest! Second, write them down, and keep your list where you can find it. Third, read through your list every time you edit. It will remind you which kinds of errors are most likely to spoil the polish on your writing.

An Honest Look in the Writer's Mirror

If this checklist is going to be truly personal (and it will be useful only if it is), you will have to be honest with yourself about your writing. To start, take a close look at one or two pieces of writing from your folder. As you read through these pieces, list the editing problems that seem to pop up most frequently. Remember to look and listen closely for mistakes.

Read your work out loud—every word. What do you notice? Do you see any missing punctuation? Letters you didn't capitalize before? A place where you started a new paragraph but shouldn't have? Extra or missing words? These are all editing problems that should be on your list. How long does your list need to be? Long enough to include all the things you know you need to look out for. It's OK if you don't need to fill in every line, but be sure to write down your main editing problems.

My Personalized Editing Checklist

1. _____
2. _____
3. _____
4. _____
5. _____
6. _____
7. _____
8. _____

Share and Compare

When you've completed your list, share it with a partner. Don't forget that these are personalized lists, so they will probably look different. For a moment though, focus on the similarities. Put a small check mark next to any editing problem that appears on both lists. It's important to know that you're not the only person working on a particular editing problem.

The Incredible Shrinking List

You've put some effort into creating the list. Now put it to good use every time you write. You may even need to have more than one copy—one at home and one in your notebook or writing folder. Each time you think you've conquered a problem (let's say you haven't seen it in the last three papers you've written), check it off your list. Eventually, your list will begin to shrink! Be careful, though! A checklist works only if you check off editing problems that you have actually "repaired." (Some students like to check, check, check, even if nothing has been fixed. Hey—you're not one of those students, are you?)

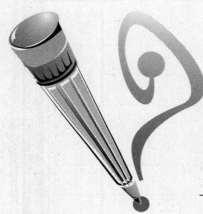

A Writer's Question

Make a prediction: Which item on your list do you think will be the first to disappear? Which one may stick around for awhile?

_____

_____

_____

Wrap-up Activity 1

EgoMania

Picture the six traits talking and bragging about their personal strengths. Read each description and put an **X** by the name of the trait that you think is speaking.

1. "I'm the trait that makes writing look splendid on the page! Without me, punctuation would be tossed everywhere—like clutter in the living room! Spelling would be sloppy—a missing letter here, the wrong letter there. Capital letters could be left in the dust. I shudder to think what writing might turn into if I weren't around to set things straight."

   ___ Ideas   ___ Conventions

   ___ Voice   ___ Sentence Fluency

2. "I give writing its energy and its appeal. I give it life. Without me, writing is pointless, lifeless, and dull. I have a thousand different personalities. I am every writer's inner thoughts and feelings. I can be sad and wistful, spirited and full of zest, or hysterically funny. Readers love me because I make them laugh and cry. Oh, yes, I'm definitely everyone's favorite trait."

   ___ Ideas   ___ Sentence Fluency

   ___ Conventions   ___ Voice

3. "I should be named "Trait of the Year." I enter every piece of writing the way important people enter a room—with a big fanfare, so people notice. I leave the same way, giving everyone something to think about. When I'm around, sentences, paragraphs, and ideas come to attention. Order is my specialty."

   ___ Voice   ___ Word Choice

   ___ Organization   ___ Conventions

4. "I am the king of originality! I never repeat myself—unless I fall into the hands of a lazy writer. I am crazy for verbs! Oh, yes, a lot of writers love adjectives, but it's powerful verbs that have launched me to greatness. At one time, I hung out with some rather dull characters—*Nice, Great, Special,* and *Stuff.* A rather weak bunch. Now I'm into verbs and sensory language."

___ Word Choice   ___ Voice

___ Organization   ___ Sentence Fluency

5. "I sing! I flow! I move with grace! I dance across the page. It isn't just how I look; it's how I sound that will capture your heart. I find ingenious ways to begin and end sentences, and I can create natural-sounding dialogue. It's hardly an exaggeration to say that I am the most important of the traits since, without me, writing would hardly be readable. Ms. Smooth—that's my nickname."

___ Word Choice   ___ Sentence Fluency

___ Ideas   ___ Conventions

6. "When it comes to important features of writing, I am the trait to beat. I've been called the heart and soul of good writing. After all, I carry the message! It helps, of course, that I hang out with Details—a hugely popular character. In addition, I'm as flexible as an Olympic gymnast. I can shift from telling a story to explaining how to change a tire in the blink of an eye. Without me, writing would be boring and hard to understand. I'm more than important. I'm vital."

___ Conventions   ___ Organization

___ Sentence Fluency   ___ Ideas

Wrap-up Activity 2

Making a Diagnosis

A filmmaker enters the editing room, looking at shots of a film she's working on. As she watches the rough cuts, she thinks to herself, "This chase sequence is too long. . . . We have too much action in this part and not enough dialogue. . . . This isn't working. . . . "

This filmmaker is making a diagnosis—figuring out what the problems are before the movie is in its final form. She will change some things before the film goes to the theaters so that it will be better than the rough cuts. She will **revise** to make the movie better. Writers revise for much the same reason: to make their writing more readable and interesting for the intended audience.

Read the four writing samples, each of which needs revision. Diagnose the main problem for each piece of writing. Circle *a, b, c,* or *d.* Write your own comments, too. (**Note:** A piece could have more than one problem, but one kind of problem should really stand out.)

Sample 1

So I am not that great of a cook, right? But my mom asked me to make a birthday cake for my sister's birthday because she did not have time to make it herself. My mom works. She is a school counselor. This is so weird because I am not such a great cook. I don't know much about cakes and stuff. So I got out all the stuff you need and followed the directions and everything. It was not that easy because it was my first cake, but I got through it all right. It wasn't a great cake or anything but it turned out all right. Everyone said it tasted pretty good even though it looked kind of weird because of the frosting. The candles were really nice, and we had gifts and stuff, so mostly it was a great party. I hope that is the last time I have to bake cake for a long time.

The MAIN problem with Sample 1 is

    a. Ideas: The writer jumps from topic to topic with no clear main idea.

    b. Conventions: The large number of spelling and punctuation errors makes this piece hard to follow or understand.

    c. Organization: If you put these sentences in a different order, they would make a great story.

    d. Word Choice: The writing does not paint a clear picture because many words are vague or repeated.

My thoughts about Sample 1: _____

_____

_____

Sample 2

    This was the year I thought I would learn to cross country ski I did not realize how difficult it could be. It is hard to keep your balance. It is also very tiring. I tried for over an hour just to keep my balance I kept landing face first right in the snow! I did not think it was very funny but my friends kept laughing so hard I thought they would never stop. I think it is one of the hardest things I have tried on my third try though I was able to stay up for more than a minute! I guess that proves if you stick with something hard enough, you can do it!

The MAIN problem with Sample 2 is

    a. Ideas: It is very hard to tell what the writer is talking about.

    b. Organization: The paper has no real introduction or conclusion.

    c. Sentence Fluency: Some sentences are short and choppy while others are run-ons; in addition, many begin with "I" or "It."

    d. Voice: The writer is clearly very bored with this topic and puts no energy into the writing.

My thoughts about Sample 2: _____

_____

_____

Sample 3

On one of our school field trips we went to an art museum. I forget where it was. We just walked around and stuff, and this guy explained some of the art, like where it was from and different things the artists were thinking when they did the sculpture or painted the picture or whatever. He asked us to think about whether we would like to be artists, and if we would, what kind of art we found the most interesting. In the front hall of the museum there was a little model of some of the pyramids from Ancient Egypt. I didn't see the point of it since they looked just like the real pyramids except they were very small, of course. The trip took a really long time. My feet hurt the whole time. Then we had lunch at a fast food restaurant. I had four tacos because I was really hungry.

The MAIN problem with Sample 3 is

a. **Voice:** The writer puts almost no feeling or energy into this paper.

b. **Sentence Fluency:** Almost all the sentences begin the same way, plus there are way too many run-on sentences.

c. **Conventions:** The writer misspells a lot of words and uses way too many commas.

d. **Sentence Fluency:** If some of the details were moved around and the paper started with the part about the pyramids, it would be much easier to follow.

My thoughts about Sample 3: _____

_____

_____

Sample 4

A lot of kids get in trouble at school, but I think my brother is something of a champ at it. He never does anything really terrible, like wrecking school property or injuring people. His specialty is strange experiences that would never happen to other people in a million years. Once at a track meet, he lost one of his shoes. It just flew off his foot, and we never did find it. Now this was a total accident, but the coach was not too happy about it, especially since you can't leap hurdles very well in one stocking foot. Another time, his lunch exploded. It was really my mom's fault because she sent a whole can of instant whipping cream to school. Whose mother does this? Anyhow, my brother shook it up too much before squirting it on his fudge brownie and ended up decorating the whole lunchroom ceiling. Everybody but the principal loved it. Last week he shut the bottom of his tee shirt in his locker and then forgot the combination to his lock, so he had the choice of slipping out of the shirt or being late to class. Which choice do you think he made? The math teacher didn't think it was very funny having Brandon walk in without a shirt, but the other kids thought it was hysterical. It held up the lesson for about ten minutes, so now Brandon has to write an essay on proper school conduct. Like he would know!

The MAIN problem with Sample 4 is

a. **Word Choice:** Many words are repeated and the writer uses almost no verbs at all.

b. **Ideas:** The writer uses almost no details to help us picture the kinds of things Brandon does in school.

c. **Organization:** The paper is easy to follow up to the end, but it stops very abruptly without much of a conclusion.

d. **Voice:** The writing is pretty flat because the writer sounds so bored with his story about Brandon.

My thoughts about Sample 4: _____

_____

_____